LIGHT
Your Path to Success

Lessons in Leadership & Coaching

by
John Sattem

Copyright © 2021 by John Sattem.
All rights reserved.
This book is protected under the copy right laws of the United States of America. Any reproductions or other unauthorized use of the material herein is prohibited without the express written permission of the author.

Cover design by Kelly Laine Designs

ISBN 979-8-9851000-1-3 (paperback)
ISBN 979-8-9851000-2-0 (hardcover)
ISBN 979-8-9851000-0-6 (eBook)

Dedication

I dedicate this book to all the people who have touched my life as coaches and mentors along my path. Your gifts of wisdom, time, and encouragement have allowed me to be the person I am today. You are the inspiration for this book, and it is my hope that what you have shared with me will be the LIGHT to guide others on their path to success.

Acknowledgments

A big thank you to so many people who have loved, supported, and encouraged me to keep taking my shot in life.

My wife, Alisa, is my best friend and partner. I love how we share so many of these stories. You are smart and talented. I enjoyed being able to co-write with you to get your perspective. I love you so much!

My son, Steven, thinks big but has an even bigger heart. My daughter, Emily, I admire for being wiser than her age.

My mom and dad were my earliest coaches and have given me a lifetime of love and support. My brother, Brian, has been my best friend growing up, and we continue to share a passion for outdoor activities. My talented sister, Kathy, shared her writing expertise through invaluable coaching on becoming an author. She has been such a big help editing, and I am so grateful for her expert guidance. Inviting her to collaborate on this project not only made the book so much better, but it helped grow our relationship along the way.

I am grateful for all the people who have given their time, wisdom, gifts, and love to help me become the person I am today. I am a work in progress, but I will always be grateful for how you have shaped me as a person.

A special thank you to Rich Blazevich, who is my writing coach, accountability partner, and friend. Without your coaching and encouragement, this dream of becoming a published author would not be possible. For anyone who has a story to tell and wants to write a book, Rich is the person you want by your side.

I am grateful for all the people who have invested their time, talents, wisdom, and their LIGHT along my path so I can be a better version of myself.

Table of Contents

Introduction 1
Learn from Everyone 5
    Chapter 1: Early Coaches 7
    Chapter 2: Don't Judge a Book 19
    Chapter 3: Bad Bosses 27
Inspire Collaboration 35
    Chapter 4: Create a Winning Culture 37
    Chapter 5: Personal Board of Directors 45
Grow Your Knowledge and Skills 51
    Chapter 6: Early Jobs 53
    Chapter 7: Lessons from Fishing 65
    Chapter 8: Mentoring 73
    Chapter 9: Setbacks 83
Healthy Relationships Matter 93
    Chapter 10: Less Boozing, More Moving 95
    Chapter 11: Coach's Tips 103
Take Your Shot 113
    Chapter 12: Keep Taking Your Shot 115
    Chapter 13: Interviewing 125
    Chapter 14: The Girl in High School 139
Closing Thoughts 155
About the Author 157

Introduction

Are you struggling to find success in your life? Maybe you're not sure how to confidently navigate difficult situations at work. We all encounter challenges like that at times. I know I have. Progress and success come from knowing how to manage those moments.

This book is your invitation to learn and grow from some of my life lessons in leadership and coaching. May you find insight, inspiration, and encouragement in these stories to move you closer to where you want to be.

A key to being successful is to LIGHT your path along the way:

Learn From Everyone

Invite Collaboration

Grow Your Knowledge and Skills

Healthy Relationships Matter

Take Your Shot

The LIGHT often comes from coaches who play a vital role in our lives. They serve as guides who teach us valuable skills, lessons, and habits that contribute to our character and help shape how we approach the world.

Everyone has coaches in life, whether it's a parent, boss, teacher, clergy member, or friend. Coaches can come and go, and sometimes we don't realize that someone has served as a coach until after the fact.

I have been extremely fortunate with the coaches I have had in my life. My parents were excellent coaches when I was young, my high school basketball coach was invaluable during my formative years, and I have had friends and colleagues later in life who still serve as my coaches.

I attribute much of the success in my 32 years of sales and leadership roles in a Fortune 100 company to my coaches. I also attribute the strength and happiness of my personal relationships to lessons I've learned from being coached.

Not only is it important to identify the coaches in your life but equally important is to learn how to be coachable and apply what you have learned. A strong leader must be able to do both—coach and be coached.

This book is for any stage of your life when you are seeking growth in either your professional or personal life. It took me many years to become a servant leader, and it's still a work in progress.

Continuous development not only makes you more impactful at work, but it also helps evolve you into the best version of yourself. Gain from my experiences, ideas, and tips for how you can be a better leader and coach in your own life and for others.

The chapters in each section will include stories and examples to illustrate different principles of LIGHT. At the end of each chapter, there are reflection questions to inspire thought or action on your part. You will see how to identify growth opportunities and apply each principle of LIGHT on your path to success.

As I have gone through my own journey in life, I have become aware that you need to be open, vulnerable, and face gaps you may have to enable successful learning and growth. LIGHT up the parts of your path that you want to improve or make better. It can make you feel nervous, anxious, and a little overwhelmed. But when you LIGHT those areas, you can see the path forward toward where you want to go.

Enjoy this journey and LIGHT your path to be happy and successful.

Learn from Everyone
I
G
H
T

Chapter 1: Early Coaches

Everyone has had coaches and can be a coach. It doesn't matter where you live, your education level, or your profession.

My family came from very humble beginnings. I was born in Chicago while my dad was going to dental school and my mom was an elementary school teacher. My parents emphasized hard work, the importance of education, doing more with less, not wasting, and having a vision.

My parents both grew up in Peoria, Illinois. My dad entered the Air Force as a dentist and was stationed at Offutt Air Force Base outside of Omaha, Nebraska. They liked the Midwest values and its lifestyle and decided to raise their family in Omaha and start a dental practice there.

I am the oldest of three children in my family. My brother, Brian, is one of my best friends. We both loved playing neighborhood sports year-round: front yard tackle football in the fall, big ball baseball at our friend's farm in the summer, and basketball in the driveway all year long. As we got older, our dad took us fishing, hunting, and golfing. These early activities turned into lifelong passions for both of us and our families. We have learned from our mom and dad to share our love and passion for these activities with our kids. The most important thing isn't the activity; it's the connection and bond that comes from them.

My sister, Kathy, is the youngest sibling. Kathy played sports, danced, and went fishing with us, but she has always been more artistic. She has an amazing ability to write. She writes children's books and is a writer and editor for a local magazine.

Kathy has been so helpful to me as I have gone down this path of writing my first book. I have a much greater appreciation for her skills and talents in the writing world. I have found writing is not easy, but it's very rewarding, and Kathy has shared her passion with me.

We lived in a modest split-level home. My dad started his dental practice, and my mom helped by running the office and managing the books. It was evident early on that my parents were great partners in life. They were connected in all phases of running a business and raising a family, which were two of the first lessons they taught me.

As I reflect on my formative years, three people clearly stand out in my mind who served as my earliest coaches: my mom, my dad, and my high school basketball coach, Tom Hall.

Expectations

One of the best lessons I learned from my mom was the value of setting expectations. She grew up in a small town near Peoria, Illinois. She came from a hard-working, blue-collar family and had to work hard for everything she gained. Education was very important to her.

My mom had a neighbor, Mrs. Gove, who one day said, "You would be a very good teacher." My mom never considered that prior to that day, but those words of encouragement set her on a path of becoming a teacher. You never know who will say something that creates an inner spark in you.

My mom was the valedictorian of her high school class. She was also the first person from her family to go to college, and she had to pay for her education by working summers and during the school year to supplement her academic scholarships. She majored in education and went on to become an elementary school teacher in Chicago. She has been a teacher her entire life in and out of the classroom.

My mom always expected her kids to give their best in school and set a high bar for us. I was an above-average student. Not the top of my class, but I did well in classes I enjoyed and only average in the classes I found less interesting.

One of my favorite classes in middle school was algebra. I wasn't very good at it or all that interested in it, but the teacher found a way to be funny and engaging, and I did well in that class.

I remember a cold January night in Omaha. I was studying for my Spanish test the next day and struggled with some of the material. I knew I wasn't going to do well on the test. I decided I needed to set the expectation for my mom that I wasn't going to end up with an "A" in the class. It might have been some of my early "selling skills" coming into play.

I casually let my mom know I was not understanding the material, and it looked like my grade was going to be in the "B" or possibly "C" range. We sat down on the couch, and she asked what I was struggling with and if I had talked to my teacher about it. I told her that I didn't fully understand the material, but I had not talked to my teacher.

Excellence in my mind meant getting the "A." I thought that was my mom's definition as well. I was surprised to learn otherwise.

She wanted "A's" for her kids, but her measurement for success was effort. Was I giving my best effort? Was I asking for help?

She suggested I speak with my teacher the next morning and let him know where I needed some help. As she stood up from the couch, she said, "John, I'm not worried about your grade as long as I know you put in your best effort."

I didn't get the "A" that semester, but I did have a better understanding of what was expected, and it was much bigger than a grade in middle school Spanish.

When someone sets an expectation for you, whether it's a parent, a boss, or a significant other, what really matters is giving your best effort. It's important to ask what the expectations are upfront so both parties are clear. It's also important to set expectations for others, especially if you lead a team. Writing expectations down is a way to ensure everyone understands them and can refer to those expectations when they aren't being met. But if you are giving your best effort, better results will follow.

Hard Work

Any good coach emphasizes the importance of hard work to master a skill, and that's one of the lessons my dad taught me.

My dad grew up in Peoria, Illinois. His father, my grandfather- Norman Sattem, was a senior executive at Caterpillar Tractor Company. My dad was exposed to other senior executives and their families during this time and saw what was required to be successful. He learned the value of a good education, working hard, investing, and always improving.

My dad also grew up playing basketball, so it was an early common interest we had. When he was growing up, he practiced in his driveway. The basketball rim was attached to a power pole, so it was a very bare-bones setup.

Since the driveway surface was gravel, he couldn't dribble without the ball bouncing away. Instead of becoming a great dribbler, he focused on being an excellent shooter. He practiced for hours, shooting from all different spots on the driveway.

Away from basketball, my dad was a serious student and a hard worker. He had a Latin teacher in high school who was very kind to him, and he has always appreciated that trait in people. It's probably why he has a soft spot for golden retrievers. They are such kind dogs.

My dad operated heavy construction equipment in the summers during college so he could help pay his tuition and living expenses while in school. He continued to stay focused as he and my mom built a successful dental practice. My parents earned everything they have the old-fashioned way—hard work and sacrifice. They are some of my earliest coaches and have always been my best cheerleaders my entire life.

One of the best days in my early childhood was when my dad announced we were getting our very own basketball hoop for our driveway. The day it arrived, we dug a hole, put the basketball pole in the ground, and poured concrete to secure it. I wrote my initials in the concrete before it dried. My dad had kept his old basketball rim from his driveway and attached it to the backboard on the pole in our driveway. That rim had seen a lot of shots over two generations. My dad installed a floodlight and shined it toward the basket so we could play at night. With that one light, I practiced with only the rim being visible as I took my shot over and over.

You could always find me outside in any weather, practicing basketball and trying to improve. I shoveled snow, picked at ice, and braved below-freezing temperatures to practice. To my mother's chagrin, I learned that you could put a cold basketball in the dryer and warm it so it would bounce in the arctic temperatures. I would put one basketball in the dryer while I practiced outside. Then, when the ball I was practicing with would become too cold to bounce properly, I would swap to the warm ball that was in the dryer. What I didn't factor in was the loud thud the ball made inside the dryer, making it sound like it could explode at any minute. My mom quickly put an end to that experiment.

My dad has excellent hand-eye coordination and always instructed me to aim just beyond the rim as my target on the basket. He always encouraged me to learn one new move each season to become a better player. I took my dad's advice. I spent countless hours on the driveway making up scenarios that could happen in a game. I would imagine the clock counting down and taking the game-winning shot. I would imagine I got fouled and had to make two free throws to tie the game and go into overtime. I would imagine having two people guarding me and taking an off-balance shot to win the game.

My dad came home from work most nights at the same time. I would be in the driveway practicing, and he'd ask what new move I was working on. I told him what I was trying, and he'd ask to see me do it.

As I was getting older, the opposing players were getting taller and faster, and I had to create new ways to get my shot off without being blocked. One summer, I was working on faking one direction, crossing over the other side, and taking a shot from a more open space. I practiced that move over and over until I could do it without thinking. At first, it was slow, awkward, and clumsy. I would fake left, cross over to my right, elevate for the shot, and then follow through with my hand aimed at the rim. Day after day, week after week, month after month, all summer long, I practiced that move. Each day my dad would ask, "How is it going?"

I felt it getting easier and easier. I started practicing the move in summer league games and saw how it was improving my game. Later in the year, during actual games when the circumstances were right, I was able to pull it off. Fake left, cross over, elevate, take the shot, and follow through. Swish! The ball went straight through the net. I looked up in the stands and saw my dad clap on the play. It felt great to be able to finally see it pay off. That would never have happened without putting in the hard work to master the skill and without the consistent encouragement from my dad.

The reason good coaches stress the importance of hard work is because they know it will build your confidence and result in success. As a young person in their career or someone starting a new position, hard work is essential to not only learn a new skill, but also to be able to easily repeat it. As a leader, it's important to always encourage your team to work hard every step of the way.

Consistent, hard work is always needed to achieve your goals in whatever your passion may be.

Perseverance

One of the most important lessons I learned from one of my early coaches was perseverance. By never giving up, you become stronger and can overcome adversity.

My high school basketball coach was "old school." He was a great technical coach, an excellent play-caller, and demanded the best from you, but if you messed up or didn't give your best, he was going to let you know about it in no uncertain terms. He had a way of getting your attention to "do better and fix it." It never felt good in the moment, but you knew you had to improve or you weren't going to see much playing time until your skills or effort improved. At the heart of it, you also knew he loved and cared about his players and teams.

I knew my high school coach for over eight years -- from elementary school until I graduated from high school. He hosted a summer basketball camp every June for four weeks. My mom signed me up for the first two-week session of camp going into the summer of fourth grade. During those first few days, I loved the camp. The coaches put us through drills, and then we got to practice our skills each day during scrimmages or practice games. Toward the end of the first two-week session, I found out they had another two-week session, and at the end of the four weeks, they gave out awards. Was I good enough to win an award? Intrigued, I wanted to attend the second session to find out.

I asked my mom if I could attend the next session. She said she would talk it over with my dad. I didn't understand the hesitation but waited for the answer. What I didn't know at the time was that money was tight. This wasn't in the budget, and the first session was a stretch for them, not to mention my mom was going to have to drop me off and pick me up every day for two more weeks.

A couple of days later, my mom let me know that I could attend the next session. I was so excited! However, I was going to have to increase my chores around the house and do some extra work in the yard. No problem. I also needed to find a friend to join me in the second session, and that friend's family would have to split the pick-up and drop-off duties with my mom. Now that was a little more difficult because I was going to have to recruit a friend, and he was going to have to convince someone in his family to drive us half the time. When you want something bad enough, you try to figure it out, and I was determined.

I asked a few friends, but it didn't work because they couldn't find someone in their family to split carpooling. Time was running out to sign up. I asked someone I didn't know very well if they were attending the second session. They said yes but needed someone to share rides. What a find! We both found a schedule that worked, and the second session was a go.

The second session was like the first, but it included more formal contests as a part of the camp routine. They had contests for free throws, a one-on-one bracket where you advanced by the first player hitting five baskets, the best defender awards, and the best player awards for each grade. I worked hard, took in each coaching session, and did my best with each contest. I improved every day.

The last day of camp arrived on that final hot day in June. Toward the end of that last day, Coach blew his whistle and we all gathered in the center of the gym floor. Coach started handing out awards for each grade, which were typed certificates. The last award was for the best player in each grade. Because I was in the youngest age group, we were first. My heart raced as Coach stood up to hand out the best player award. He said the best player in the fourth-grade group was…John Sattem. I was so proud! I walked up, accepted that sheet of paper, and knew basketball was a true love and passion of mine. I was so excited to share the news with my parents that night.

As the years went by, that basketball camp became less about the awards and more about the relationships with the other players and coaches. Eventually, I was able to become a coach for the younger players and pay it forward by helping them build their skills and see them gain confidence in their game.

Perseverance is a trait that every professional needs. There will always be mistakes, failures, and doubts, but having the ability to push through them and keep going is key to being successful. You also need to lead by example and show others the importance of perseverance so when a team experiences a setback, they'll know it's only temporary, and everyone must keep moving forward.

Summary

Learning from others is not always a formal process. It can come from casual conversations on a couch or in a driveway. Family and friends are a wealth of insight and knowledge. The LIGHT they share from their own life experiences and successes is a resource to be tapped into and built upon. Put into practice what they teach and keep practicing those skills.

Ask people in your professional and personal life to clearly define their expectations of you and do the same for others. Once those expectations are set and agreed upon, then you can apply the hard work needed on a regular basis to meet them and hopefully exceed them. Working hard day in and day out shows that you have the perseverance to continue to see a goal through until it's met. When you have all three of these traits working in conjunction, you develop the confidence to do it repeatedly, and that's when true success happens.

Chapter Questions

1. Who were your earliest coaches? What impact did they have on you? What did you learn from them? How does that manifest itself today? Have you let them know the impact they have had on your life? If not, reach out and let them know.
2. How can you bring out the best in your performance? What motivates you to achieve your goals? Who pushes you to be your best?

3. If you aren't getting what you need out of your career or life, what needs to change? Who can you find to help LIGHT up those areas for you?
4. Who are you coaching or impacting so that you can be someone's positive role model in life? How are you paying it forward?

Chapter 2: Don't Judge a Book ...

Sometimes you meet somebody in life who leaves a bigger impact on you than most. When that happens, it's important to recognize it and be grateful the interaction occurred. You need to cherish and nurture those people and let them know the impact they have had on you. It's also important to reflect on why they had an impact and what lesson you can carry forward.

This happened to me one late summer afternoon in a college gymnasium at a summer basketball camp in Hastings, Nebraska. I had heard about this basketball camp for several years. Some of the older high school players talked about it. Kids from across the Midwest attended to work on skills, play against some of the best players in the region, and be seen by college coaches.

I talked to my parents about registering, but it was considerably more expensive than the local high school camp I had been going to for many summers. Attending the camp required staying overnight in the dorms, eating on campus, and playing basketball all day and into the evenings. I really wanted to attend to see how I stacked up against some of the best players in my region.

My parents agreed to split the cost with me. I started mowing lawns and doing odd jobs for neighbors. I didn't particularly like the work, but it was a means to an end to reach my goal. By mid-summer, I had earned enough to enroll in the camp and reserve my spot. I packed my bag and threw in my pillow. I was nervous and excited. I had never been to a college campus other than for a Nebraska football game.

My dad drove me from Omaha to Hastings and dropped me off at registration. I made my way to the sign-in desk, was assigned a dorm and a roommate, and was told to report at 5 PM for camp introductions and open gym.

I got my key and found my room. It had two beds, two desks, and two chairs. Dorm rooms have changed a lot since those days. I changed into my basketball gear and headed down to the gym with the rest of the campers. There were over 200 kids in the gym. We practiced shooting, sized each other up as competition, and got a feel for how things were going to work for the upcoming week.

Looks Can Be Deceiving

I noticed a tall player with a unique gait entering the gym. At first glance, he looked like the other players, but after a closer look, I realized he only had one arm! I assumed he must be a coach because obviously, you couldn't play basketball with only one arm. Boy, was I wrong about that!

I watched him warm up and knew I needed to meet him. I walked up, reached out to shake his hand, and introduced myself. He turned to shake my hand with his left hand and said, "Hi, my name is Ron, but you can call me Gus." His entire hand swallowed mine in that clasp.

At the far end of the gym stood a basket that you could raise up and down to various heights called the SkyDunk machine. The younger campers lowered it to get the feel of a power dunk, and the older campers raised it above the standard 10 feet to see how high they could dunk the ball. Gus grabbed the basketball with one hand like a grapefruit. He palmed the ball with each dribble and held it in his hand like the ball was on an invisible string. He started toward the basket, cradled the ball against his body to maintain control, leaped off the ground, and slammed the ball through the basket—all with one hand. It was amazing.

During the week, Gus and I squared off during scrimmages. He was an excellent player. He had a lot of natural strength, which was the result of working on his family farm. His shot was textbook. He had a long, smooth extension of his arm, and the ball would be on target because he didn't have his other hand to get in the way of the arc of the ball. When he missed, it was almost always long or short. Rarely would he miss left or right.

The other thing I noticed about Gus was his work ethic. When camp drills were done for a session, he always stayed longer. Gus shot free throws for hours, honing his skills. I asked him why he spent so much time practicing. He said he didn't want his farm accident, which caused the loss of his arm, to be an excuse for not being a great player. It was one of the first times in my life I watched someone make the most out of their situation rather than feel sorry for themselves. It was a lesson that always stuck with me.

Don't Rest on Your Wins

The camp held numerous contests during the week, including a one-on-one competition. The first to reach a certain score advanced to the next contest, and once you lost, you were out. I was in the opposite bracket as Gus and met him in the finals.

All the campers gathered around the court to watch us in the championship match.

Gus was a really tough opponent because he was so much stronger than me. He backed his body into me and then created space to find an opening for his shot. I relied on my quickness to maneuver around him and drive to the basket or fake a drive and pull up for a jump shot.

The game was tight and back and forth. I finally had the ball and the lead by one and could win the game on my next possession. I faked my shot, crossed over my step, and made my way to the basket. I went up for an easy shot when I felt Gus come over me and block my shot with his massive mitt for a hand.

Gus had the ball next. He waved it in his grip when I saw an opening and slapped the ball away to gain my final possession. I knew I had to change my tactics on the next possession. I faked a drive to my left, stopped, and pulled up for my shot. Gus recovered, elevated with me, and I barely got the ball over his outstretched hand. The ball arched toward the basket and swished through the net. Game over…at least for now.

That next season I stayed in touch with Gus either by phone or by reading about his games in the newspaper. I tracked how many points he scored in his games. He did the same with me. This was long before the internet, and the only device we had to stay connected with was a phone with a cord.

Gus and I wanted to take our games to the next level and decided the next summer we would attend basketball camp at our largest state university to see how we matched up with even better competition. At this camp, we were roommates in the dorm, and I got to know Gus even better. I learned to appreciate so many of the things he had to overcome due to his injury. I saw the physical scars on his arm and knees from the accident and the mental strength it took to overcome it. We take for granted everything we can do with two limbs. Imagine trying to tie your shoelaces with one hand or button a shirt. Gus did all of that and had such a positive attitude about it.

Determination Over Talent

At that year's camp, Gus and I competed in the one-on-one semi-finals. Once again, it was a close game. We knew each other's strengths and go-to moves. Gus also had a year of paybacks in the making.

We played on the center court. This time it was in the college arena, which could hold 14,000 fans. I started out with the lead and discovered my shot was on. Gus kept taking me down low toward the basket where he could use his body as leverage and get his shot off closer to the basket.

In the end, Gus had the ball. He faked to his left and then stopped. He took a slight step back, and with his one arm, he squared the ball to the basket and let it fly. Based on the ball's arc, I knew it was going to be good. Nothing but net! Gus won and evened things up from our contest the summer before. I was disappointed but only for a moment. My friend was going to the finals the next day.

That morning, Gus woke up extra early. I knew he was dialed in and ready to go. He played pump-up music from our big boom box stereo with a mixtape of his favorite songs. Gus was going up against a kid who was 6'8" and had multiple Division I scholarship offers. Gus didn't have any scholarship offers. It was going to be a tough match-up because his opponent had a great shot from the perimeter, was able to use his height, and also go down low by the basket for some easy, short shots.

Gus's opponent got out to an early lead. Gus hadn't found a good strategy to score on him. Things were not looking good. He was down six points in a game that only went to 21. He was frustrated and visibly angry.

Then things started to click. He used his strength and quick first step to drive to the basket hard, fending off the taller player with his right side. He made some great moves to the basket and tied up the score. Gus was the crowd favorite, and the other campers pulled for him. At the end of the contest, Gus swiped at the ball and knocked it away with his large hand. Gus stood just above the free-throw line with the opportunity to win the game. He took the ball in his hand, faked a 17-foot jump shot, and then like the ball was on a string, he brought it back, took two dribbles to his left, and went in for a layup over the outstretched arm of his opponent. Gus won! I couldn't have been happier for him. I gave Gus a high five, and he just smiled. I knew how badly he wanted to win to show that he could match up with the best, even with one arm. It was his determination that won him that competition.

Recently, I had the opportunity to sit down with Gus and relive some of those stories growing up and playing together those summers in high school. We are a lot older and slower, but maybe a little wiser now. We have grown kids who are making their own way in life. You know you have a friend for life when you don't see each other for a period of time, and you pick right back up where you left off. Those are special relationships. Don't take them for granted. Do your best to stay connected when you form a relationship like that. They don't come around very often.

Summary

Peers and friends offer LIGHT and motivation to you throughout life. When I think back on my friendship with Gus, it always serves as a reminder that I can't predict how things are going to turn out. He challenged me to be better.

People's strengths or what they are trying to overcome may not be initially evident. It's important to be mindful not to judge someone by their physical appearance or traits and never limit how much someone can achieve, including yourself. Don't rest on your latest achievements or be frustrated with a setback. Always push to do better. Hard work, drive, and determination will take you far in life, even farther than sheer talent alone. Look for those natural traits in others. Surrounding yourself with people with strong drive and determination will motivate you and brighten your path. A sign of a confident leader is someone who knows their limitations and surrounds themselves with people who have other talents and skills.

Chapter Questions

1. When have you judged someone when you first met? Were you able to find out more about them and change your perspective? How can you be more open in the beginning?

2. What challenges are you facing in your life? How are you coping and adapting? Asking for help is a sign of strength, not weakness.
3. Have you found a life-long friend? How are you nurturing and growing that relationship? When was the last time you connected with that person? We all need to connect with and care for people who have had a profound impact on our lives.

Chapter 3: Bad Bosses

In my career, I have had excellent bosses, leaders, and direct managers. They have helped me become the person I am today. However, along the way, I have had some bad bosses, too. While I didn't enjoy those experiences, I did learn some valuable lessons. If you are in that situation, all is not lost. Learn what you would do differently when you become a manager or leader.

The one good thing about having a bad boss is it doesn't last forever. Eventually, one of you will move on. If your manager is not treating you with respect or their behavior is ethically wrong, then you need to report that to the human resources department or someone with authority in your organization. The days of "that's just the way it is" are definitely over.

Leadership Matters

Early in my career, I was promoted and had a new manager in a new city. I was excited about this new opportunity. I was given more responsibility with larger customers and felt like I was growing as a sales executive. I walked into my new boss's office for one of our first meetings. He gave me a stack of customer files from the previous salesperson and told me to read through all the files and come back with a plan to call on these customers. I didn't have specific training for my new role or anyone assigned to help me transition. I was left to figure it out.

I took the files, headed to my cubicle, and began trying to piece things together. I sorted my customers by sales volume, channels of business, number of outlets, and customer office locations. I examined how we could grow the business and created a top ten opportunity list for my portfolio. I reviewed the contracts and built a flow chart for contract expiration dates for renewal. I also looked for new business opportunities in my territory.

At the end of the week, I told my boss I was ready to review my analysis and get his feedback. We set up a meeting for Friday afternoon. Shortly before our meeting, his administrative assistant let me know he was running late. I waited another two hours until we finally met. He was rushed, not focused, and clearly didn't want to have the conversation.

Two minutes into my findings, he said he wasn't very happy with my approach or my thought process. He gave me a list of things he wanted to see by Monday morning without letting me finish. I left his office and wrapped up my day with a list of items I had to prepare all weekend.

As I walked to my car, I questioned if I was cut out for this new position. But I spent the weekend preparing for Monday. Key information was missing from the files, which made it even more difficult. I finally had my assignment ready for Monday.

I arrived at work early Monday morning, hoping to catch my boss before his day got busy. During our meeting, he answered his phone several times, shuffled through papers, and was not engaged. His only comment at the end of our meeting was for me to get out into the market and "make things happen." He said if I didn't make him look good, my career would be over in short order. I went from being excited about my new job opportunity to doubting it all.

Six months later, I had my first performance review with this manager. I prepared my review, which included my accomplishments supported by metrics and how I performed within the key competencies of my role. We met on a Saturday morning because my boss had been too busy to meet during the week. He handed me the review and then left to get a cup of coffee from the break room.

As soon as I read the review with his comments, it was clear we weren't on the same page. He negated many of my accomplishments without substantiation. We had spent little time together in the field. When he returned with his coffee, he pointed out each area in which he felt I wasn't meeting expectations and told me I didn't have what it took for a long-term career with the company. He recommended I start looking for a job elsewhere.

I left devastated. I wanted to quit right then and there. I took my papers, got up from the table, and thanked him for his comments.

I thought about my career and my long-term aspirations for the remainder of the weekend. I told myself I was going to have to work at what mattered to my boss and show him I had what it took to succeed in this job. I made a point to schedule time with him in my market, making customer calls and tracking my progress together. It was not easy, but things slowly improved.

About three months after that Saturday performance review, my boss's boss called an "emergency meeting" with all the sales and marketing team members. He announced our manager was no longer with the company and we would report to him until a new manager was named.

You should always have compassion for someone when they lose their job. I also took away a key learning from that time. A good manager coaches their people to be better and does not coach them using fear or intimidation. Eventually, it all comes full circle.

Manage Weaknesses

Later in my career, when I had my first role as a people leader, I had a new manager put in place six months into my role. All I knew about him was that he was demanding and had high expectations. I also heard if you didn't make him "look good" with senior management, he made your work life difficult.

At that point in my career, I wanted my manager to know I had things under control and could manage my team well. My communication philosophy for letting my manager know what was going on in my business was "no news is good news." In my mind, that meant that my boss didn't have to get involved and could focus on other things that were more pressing with other people. I didn't share the challenges I was overcoming, successes in the field, or have regular communication. I learned the hard way that this is not an optimal approach.

I had just finished my first full year in that role and took some time off for the holidays. I felt good about what the team and I had accomplished that year, and I was looking forward to refining some of our processes and developing new strategies of growth in the portfolio. On my first day back in the new year, my boss wanted to meet offsite. It was odd for him to come into town with such short notice, but I thought it could be an opportunity to share my goals for the year.

We met at a local coffee shop. As we sat down, he pulled out a stack of papers from his briefcase. He said the meeting was an opportunity for me to improve my leadership and team performance. He outlined all the areas in which he was dissatisfied with my performance and leadership behaviors, citing specific examples. It took all my patience to actively listen. When he finished, I asked to share my point of view.

I explained my philosophy for "no news meant I was handling the things I was responsible for." It turned out he didn't share that philosophy. No news was just no news. I realized he did not know all the good things that I was doing with my team. He said I had 60 days to improve my performance, or he was going to put me on a formal plan to improve or exit the company. My back was against the wall with him, and I needed to change his perspective on my abilities and performance.

Outline Expectations

Before he left town, I asked for a detailed account of his expectations so I knew what changes to make. It no longer mattered what I thought equaled good performance, only what he considered it to be. I needed to get on board with him, or it was going to be over for me with the company.

The next morning, I made a plan. I needed to own the changes and implement them. However, I wasn't going to be able to do that on my own. I had to engage my direct team and the support team around us for help. Asking for help with my weaknesses was a sign of strength and allowed me to grow. I set up communication processes and regular check-in calls with my boss. I asked him to visit my market and attend customer calls. I also had my team create updates that could be consolidated into reports that showed progress against key selling objectives. Most importantly, I asked for regular feedback on my progress and if I was meeting his expectations.

After doing this consistently for two months, things improved. My boss stopped asking for updates outside of our regular times. I asked him for advice and guidance but clearly stated my thoughts regarding direction and strategy. He was never one of my favorite managers, but the experience of working for him taught me valuable lessons.

Don't assume your boss knows what or how you're performing. That only happens through regular communication. Make sure you understand your boss's expectations of you and their definition of success. Utilize your team and others around you to help build your communication plan and report successes and failures early and often in the process. This lesson isn't just for people early in your career. This will be a life-long approach for you to be successful. Communication allows you to get the resources and help where needed, and sharing the team's success reflects well on everyone.

Summary

You can learn valuable lessons as much from what you perceive is a bad boss as you can from a good manager. Communication starts with you, not your manager. It's important to determine your boss's definition of success and how they measure your performance. No situation lasts forever, so learn all you can during that time, whether it's wonderful or a hard experience. Your job is to grow and learn how to constantly improve.

Chapter Questions
1. Are you clear on the expectations and what success looks like from your manager's perspective? If not, take time to clarify and set up a process to share progress.
2. Does your manager understand what you need from them to be successful?
3. Have you ever been surprised by a performance review or caught off guard by a boss's feedback? Are you keeping track of your feedback from all of the people you interact with in your role? This will make a check-in or end-of-year review go much better.
4. How often do you communicate with your manager to give them progress reports where you share successes and challenges? It's up to you to align with your manager and ensure communication reaches them. You own the outcome of your career.

L
***I**nspire Collaboration*
G
H
T

Chapter 4: Create a Winning Culture

You have been on teams, groups, circles, casts, and a variety of other pods where people come together to interact. There are times when the culture is better than others. Why is that?

Everyone wants to be a part of a winning organization where the work seems easy, people understand how they contribute to the greater cause, and they have the support and freedom to do the work in which they find passion and purpose. So, what keeps getting in the way if that's what most people want every day? It comes down to one thing—leadership.

Lead by Setting Expectations

One of my mentors was a captain on a submarine in the US Navy. There were 30 subs, and after each exercise, the subs were ranked top to bottom. Each sub was built to the same specifications and staffed with the same number of crew members who were given the same orders and the same assignment. He asked if I could identify the one variable that changed their performance?

I paused to think. Then the answer became obvious: the captain of the sub. The performance of the sub and its crew depended on the captain's leadership. It was that clear and simple.

If you are a new leader or manager, how do you set the culture for your team? Culture is an interesting topic because within any organization, there can be multiple cultures. The one that will impact you the most is the culture that your direct manager creates. The other cultures matter, but the relationship between manager and employee is one of the biggest drivers of employee engagement and productivity.

I have had three experiences that have shaped how I think about and create a culture. They are from my days playing basketball, my first role as a people leader, and my last role leading a large cross-functional and matrixed organization.

As I shared earlier, my high school basketball coach's communication style was clear and direct. You knew exactly where you stood with him at every given moment. He did a great job setting expectations for effort, technique, skills, and hustle. We all knew what was expected of us.

We also knew our roles on the team. There were scorers, rebounders, defenders, and those who started and those who came off the bench. Even though we had our primary roles, everyone had to be ready to step up and fill any role at any given moment. This wasn't always easy. But our coach did a great job setting the vision for the team, which was to always give your best effort no matter what your role. Collaborating around a shared vision inspires the team to move in the same direction.

Even when the coach was yelling about effort during practice or a game, he cared about everyone playing to their potential. It was my first experience being a part of a great culture as a team member.

We played in the Class A state finals my junior season and were 23-2. But what I remember most was how well we played because everyone knew what was expected of them. Setting clear roles and expectations creates a culture that allows you to contribute and find success in your own authentic way.

Lead by Listening

Transitioning from an individual contributor to a people leader is one of the hardest transitions someone can make in their career. Many of the skills and approaches that made you successful as an individual contributor are not the path forward to being a great leader of others. It's even more difficult if you are a leader of other leaders. When you run your own portfolio or function, you set the pace, priorities, and direction. But when you do this and are leading other people, you run the risk of micromanaging, which is counterproductive. A great leader sets the vision and lets the team drive toward it.

Following an interview for a sales director position, one of the senior leaders on the interview panel shook my hand and said, "Just remember, John, that everything you have learned so far will be worthless when you start leading people."

I thought that was the craziest advice I had ever received. I had over ten years of experience in sales and customer management at that point in my career and couldn't believe he thought none of that was going to help or be valuable. There was some truth to it.

As a new people leader, I was excited to set the tone and vision for my team, as my high school basketball coach had done. I laid out very clear expectations for how I wanted things to be done. I used my own experiences as a benchmark and outlined how I wanted the team to plan and execute customer meetings. I explained goals for meeting numbers, retaining all customers, and gaining new ones in certain business categories.

I invited my new boss to my first team meeting, hoping to impress him. I began the meeting with my expectations, processes, and routines. When I asked my new team if they had any questions, they sat in silence. I took that as a good sign, so we moved on to the next topic in the agenda.

At the end of the day, my boss asked if I was open to some of his thoughts on how the day went. We sat down in my office, and he asked how I thought things went. I gave him all positive feedback. He then asked me a question I wasn't prepared for. "John, what would you do differently next time?"

I said I would like to get the team more engaged in the conversation. He then asked how I might do that? Again, I wasn't ready for the question. I made a few bumbling comments, but nothing concrete.

He said, "I want you to write down ten things you would do differently and then come up with your top three. Send those to me over the next couple of days."

As I completed that request, it dawned on me what he was doing. He was asking questions and having me come up with potential solutions versus telling me what to do. He was helping me grow and develop as a new leader. What an amazing role model and gift.

Over the next several months, I changed my approach with my vision, expectations, and routines. I asked people on the team to lead and take charge of various workstreams. I let them set the agenda and lead customer calls. At the end of a work session or customer meeting, I asked how things went and what they could do differently next time.

What I learned over many years is strong performers coached themselves. They were professional people and knew how things were going. I found myself doing a lot less "telling" and a lot more "listening." By asking questions, I could help lead them better and shine a LIGHT on a path for their success.

Lead by Inviting Collaboration

Later in my career, I was preparing to take on a role with greater influence over a cross-functional team. I would be directing a matrixed organization of over 200 people with a global scope and over $1 billion in annual top-line revenue.

I thought about how I was going to create the culture and vision for this new group I was leading. One of the main differences in this new role was that I had a direct selling organization of about 100 people, and the other half of my team reported to other functions and managers. My role was about setting the strategy and tone for the broader group.

I wanted to use my prior experiences to set the culture for my new team. I recalled how my high school basketball coach set high expectations for the team while still showing us he loved us as individuals. I thought about my early days as a people leader and how making mistakes helped me grow. Those early experiences helped LIGHT the path toward the culture I wanted to create and be a part of during the process. My vision for an ideal culture involved being with other people who were supportive. I wanted to be somewhere we could all be proud of when we came to work.

There is power and inspiration when you combine different points of view together. Thus, I asked a group of people from various functions, backgrounds, experiences, cultures, and roles to work on this project with me, not for me. I looked for other teams within the organization who had done similar work with their teams and had success.

Engaging my human resources counterpart, I looked for best practices from other industries or companies. We looked to some of our clients for inspiration and motivation on how they set and built their culture. I surveyed my entire organization on what the current culture looked like and what they wanted it to be. We had a baseline understanding of where things stood before we started building a new culture.

As I opened that first meeting with the culture team, I said I wanted a culture we could all be proud of. That was it. I was met with silence, not unlike my first experience as a team leader.

But what followed was different this time. People shared their ideas, suggested ways to benchmark our progress, and created a framework for how to convey the pillars of our culture. They took the collective genius and experience of that group and made it so much more than what any one person could have accomplished. At our annual summer meeting, the entire management team took the stage to share our vision, mission, and what our culture was going to stand for. It was then I realized my job was to bring in the players, set the stage, and let passionate and creative people lead the way. I was finally turning into a true servant leader after many years of thinking I had to do it all myself.

Summary

Learning from past experiences, taking the parts that worked, and eliminating the parts that didn't is a powerful framework. One of the important aspects is taking ideas or concepts that you experience and adapting them into your own authentic leadership style.

Take the concept of what someone is doing, personalize it, and make it your own. You should be open to new ideas and approaches. Engaging others for collective inspiration leads to a better outcome or product. It may take longer because you must let the process play out, but it will have a better result over time.

Chapter Questions

1. What is your current style of coaching? Are you telling people what to do or asking them questions? Giving orders is limiting because it's based on only what you know. This style of leading limits the growth potential of the person you are coaching because they don't have the opportunity to explore possibilities on their own.
2. How are you engaging your team in finding solutions to opportunities or challenges?
3. What is the culture for your team or organization? Have you allowed others to create it with you? Are the important aspects written down? Can someone easily identify your culture, and is it consistent across the organization? If not, you may have an opportunity to revisit this and create greater clarity.

Chapter 5: Personal Board of Directors

My Personal Board of Directors (PBOD) has not always been completely structured. Rather, it often comes together as a group of family members and other people I have sought based on the specific challenges or opportunities I'm facing. I actively share my goals with them and seek their advice.

Creating a more formally structured board has the benefit of getting clearer commitments from everyone involved, and it can even actively engage people throughout your life. Formalizing their roles as members of your PBOD can lead to them proactively guiding you instead of them just waiting for you to ask for help.

What Is a Personal Board of Directors?

Whether formalized or not, the purpose of your PBOD is to collaborate with a group that knows you well and is willing to shine LIGHT on your path through life. A PBOD is similar to the board of directors that many companies have that guides and provides strategic direction to the business and offers expertise based on their skills and experiences. However, there are a couple of differences.

Because a PBOD is a non-paid position, look for ways that the relationships can be mutually beneficial. Everyone can learn from each other. You also need to make sure your potential board members are willing to share their time and candid thoughts with you. You may collaborate with each of your board members on a one-on-one basis, or you may convene a total board meeting once or twice per year with all your PBOD members.

The core purpose of this group is to help provide feedback and guidance on major life decisions. Their shared thoughts and ideas will be more powerful than thinking through things on your own and enable you to make better decisions.

How Do You Select Your PBOD?

There are many criteria to consider when selecting your group. A wide range of skills and experiences provides more inspiration from which to draw. You may want people who have experienced what you are looking for in your life.

Consider people who are in a field of work that you are just starting or exploring. It's helpful to choose people with skills that align with gaps in your own skillset so you can learn how to acquire them or recognize the need to outsource those skills. You may want someone who is your cheerleader in life for when you are down or when things aren't going as expected.

The most important trait you want is honesty and mutual respect. This doesn't mean you will always need to take their advice, but it should be highly considered.

Consider people no longer living, but you know what advice they'd give. For example, two of my PBOD have passed on. One is my paternal grandfather, Norman Sattem. He was a senior executive at Caterpillar Tractor Company, and I often sought out his advice in thought and prayer during my corporate career. He was a kind and fair man. I leaned on his spirit to guide me through difficult customer or internal conversations. I know he is still looking over me today.

The other person who has passed on is my high school basketball coach, Tom Hall. I can still hear his voice telling me to work hard, never give up, and keep taking my shot in life.

These PBOD members are a good reminder to tell people the impact they have had on your life. Don't wait until they are gone and then wish you had reached out to them.

How Do You Interact with Your PBOD?

Formally ask each individual to be on your board either in person or by video chat, not via email or text. Tell them why they've been selected and what you hope to get out of the relationship. Set up some parameters for how often you anticipate reaching out to them and how long you want them to be on your PBOD. Be sure to give them an "out" if this isn't something they are comfortable with or don't have the time or expertise you are looking for.

Don't shy away from asking someone to be on your board for fear of them turning you down. If they decline your invitation, maybe it's just not the right time. Keep an open mind about your request to anyone. They will be touched that you asked. Even if not fully able to commit as a PBOD for you, they will be more aware of providing encouragement and insight to you.

If they accept, ask what they want to get out of being on your PBOD. Remember, this should be a two-way street, and everyone has something they can offer from their own experience, perspective, or skills. At first, it may be more one-sided toward you, but over time, it should become reciprocal.

Schedule your meetings ahead of time and let them know what you'd like to discuss in advance so they can prepare. It's also helpful to share your thought process and where you are in the decision-making matrix of the situation that you'd like to discuss.

You should also have a "no-fault exit" clause for either party if it's simply not working for either of you. For example, if one of your PBOD postpones multiple times, it may be a sign they may not be able to commit, so be sure to have that conversation and allow them to exit.

One-on-One or Group Meetings?

It is entirely up to you whether you want individual conversations or a group meeting. There is no right or wrong way to have your own PBOD. Simply having the benefit and insight from multiple board members helps you with connections. That's what is important.

An approach could be to convene your PBOD at a meeting early each year and outline what you want to accomplish both personally and professionally. Then throughout the year, utilize the board for big decisions in your life. At the end of the year, report on whether you accomplished what you set out to do. It's a great way to incorporate personal accountability. You can start anytime and can continuously change or tweak the approach to your own PBOD.

Summary

I have utilized and benefited from having a PBOD throughout my career. Formalizing your PBOD allows for more direct collaboration, encourages more purposeful conversations, and results in more successful outcomes. Having people you are accountable to is a great motivator.

My advice to you is just start. Do not let perfection get in the way. Be open to asking for help when it is needed or offered. Sometimes it just takes another lens or approach to help you get back on track or confirm you are indeed on the right path. Having a PBOD can help you live a fuller life.

Chapter Questions

1. Who are the go-to-people in your life today for big decisions? Will they be on your PBOD? Do you need to broaden your PBOD with people who have varying perspectives or backgrounds?
2. What advice or expertise do you think you need today?
3. What goals are you setting for yourself? What measurements do you have in place to track your progress? How are you doing on those goals today?
4. What is getting in your way if you have tried this idea but haven't pulled it off yet?
5. If gaining insight from other people is working for you, share that insight with even more people. Pay it forward.

L
I
Grow Your Knowledge and Skills
H
T

Chapter 6: Early Jobs

You never know how an early job will impact you later in life. These jobs help you grow by teaching skills about working, responsibility, and forming ideas for your profession. Sometimes early jobs will morph into your career or expose you to types of work you don't care to pursue. In both cases, you will learn valuable lessons about yourself.

My early jobs taught me many life skills. Some I used during my 32 years in corporate America, and others I'm reflecting on as I start my own consulting business and get back to my entrepreneurial roots. If you are starting out in your career, look back at what you enjoyed and why. Examine how that might relate to a future job or company you want to pursue or even a business you might want to start on your own.

Early Skills

My first job as a kid growing up in Omaha was working with my younger brother in the yard. We had a corner lot with a big yard and beautiful old trees. Unfortunately, those old trees dropped a lot of leaves in the fall. We had a Toro lawnmower, and my dad wanted us to bag the grass in black garbage bags.

On hot summer afternoons, sweat dripped down my face, itchy grass clippings stuck to my arms and hands, and we had what seemed like miles of grass to cut. After mowing, we trimmed the edges of the yard. My dad would come home after work and inspect the job we'd done. It taught me to not only meet expectations but to adhere to a schedule each week to complete the job. These were important aspects that I didn't realize were setting a foundation for my future career and would prove helpful in many situations.

As I entered middle school, my interest in fashion increased. I no longer wanted to wear Toughskin jeans from Sears with the reinforced knees. Comfort was not built into them. (I find it ironic that my younger nieces now buy jeans with holes in the knees.)

My mom said if I wanted to buy more fashionable clothes, I'd have to earn my own money to buy them, so I needed to generate some income. I couldn't drive yet, and I had limited skills. But I knew how to mow. I told my dad I wanted to start a mowing business and asked if I could use his mower, trimmer, and gas. He said if I paid for the supplies and kept the mower working, he'd let me use them.

Next, I had to find customers. I went door-to-door, introducing myself to neighbors, asking if they needed my services. Most didn't need their grass mowed. When the first interested person asked the price, I froze. I had no idea what to charge or what the going rate was. I went back home and asked my dad what I should charge. He told me I needed to be in a price range that made it easy to say yes but covered my costs and gave me a little money in my pocket. In other words, charge just enough that the person would still see value in getting some time back for other activities besides mowing their lawn.

The next time someone asked me for a bid, I asked what they thought was a fair price, and it was actually higher than what I was going to bid. I told him the price I was going to bid, but he could tip me more if he thought I was doing a good job, and I had my first customer. He did tip, but it was a good lesson on adding long-term value for your customers.

That was my first experience earning my own money. I loved the freedom of working on my own schedule, and I enjoyed cutting grass. I also wanted to find more customers.

One weekend I noticed our neighbor, a gentleman named Dr. Larsen, cutting his grass with a riding mower that had a grass catcher on the back. I walked across the street and asked him how the mower worked. He explained and offered to let me try it the following weekend. I eagerly agreed, and the following Saturday, he gave me instructions and told me how he wanted his yard cut. I climbed onto the seat, turned it on, put it in gear, and then activated the blades. It was a two-blade mower that gobbled up a yard in no time at all.

I finished his yard in about a third of the time it would have taken to use my push mower. I dumped out the grass, hosed down the mower in the driveway, and placed it back in his garage. Dr. Larsen handed me a check. I told him I couldn't take it since I was just learning how to use the mower. He insisted and asked me if I wanted to start mowing his lawn on a regular basis going forward. I agreed to it on the spot. Not only was it another great customer, but I got to know him, and he gave me great life advice along the way. You never know the impact people will have on you and how a relationship will start.

As fall approached, our backyard filled up with leaves. My brother and I raked sections of the yard, and as fast as we stuffed leaves into bags, more fell off the trees. We were about halfway done when I decided to ask Dr. Larsen if we could use his mower, and we worked out a deal—an equipment lease. It worked great.

I sucked up the leaves with the big mower, and my brother edged the yard and around the trees. Then we'd dump the leaves and rake them up for disposal. It cut our time down dramatically and picked up the leaves better than raking by hand. When my dad got home that night, he couldn't believe how great the yard looked, and he was impressed with how we divided the work between us.

I spent many years cutting Dr. Larsen's yard. Afterward, we'd sit at his kitchen table talking about life. I didn't realize it at the time, but he was an early coach of mine that reinforced the value of learning new skills.

Overcome Your Fears

Sometimes you must overcome fear to learn and grow. I am afraid of heights. I don't like the feeling of not being secure and the fear of falling. I had finished high school and was looking for a summer job. A friend of mine was painting houses for a small company with some other college-aged kids. There were several crews with a supervisor on each job, and the owner ensured all the houses were on track to finish per his bid estimates. I had never painted but knew some of the guys and thought it would be a good way to make some money before heading to college later in the summer.

I arrived at the job on a bright, sunny Monday morning and met the guys on the crew. The supervisor asked if I had any painting experience. I said no but was willing to learn.

He started me off on the back side of the house so any mistakes wouldn't be as visible until I got the hang of painting. I went to the backyard of this tall, two-story house. A ladder lay in the grass. The supervisor told me to use the ladder to reach the gutters and work my way back to the front of the house. I stared at the ladder and looked up at the gutters. It was not what I had envisioned for the job.

I extended the ladder and steadied it against the house, then retrieved a brush and paint can and slowly climbed toward the peak of the house, each step slow and deliberate. I told myself to focus on the gutters and not look down. I finally got to the point where I could reach the gutters with my brush. Then I looked down. My heart raced, my hands began to sweat, and my knees wobbled. I tried to block out my fear and focus on the job at hand.

I dipped my brush in the paint bucket and moved to the gutter when I realized I would need to lean back a little to paint the top edge of the gutter. This went against all my instincts to hang onto that ladder as tightly as possible. I eventually calmed down and switched painting with each hand to maximize my reach and coverage. I completed the section and made my way down the ladder to reposition and keep painting.

At lunchtime, the supervisor asked how things were going. I told him it was going great, and I was getting the hang of it. He told me that all the new guys start on the tallest part of the house to see if they are afraid of heights. I told him I had no problem on a ladder. I couldn't wait for the next "new" guy to start so I could get off the ladder and paint the lower and easier parts of the house. Even in a painting crew, there are benefits to seniority. You had to start at the top to get to the bottom.

The next summer, I went back to work for the small painting company and brought a good friend of mine, Jeff. We had a great time with a great crew. We worked hard but enjoyed joking and telling stories at lunch or during breaks. It was one of the first times I realized that when you have the right people on the job, you can get a lot done but still have a good time.

As the summer wound down, I talked to the owner about his business. He shared how he gained new prospects to make a bid and how he estimated the cost of a job, which included the number of people in the crew, amount of paint, prep time, and charging for extra services such as window washing.

He offered to drive me around neighborhoods to show what he looked for in a prospect. It intrigued me, and I agreed. We looked for houses with peeling or faded paint, and he'd ring the doorbell, introduce himself, and leave a business card. He let me ring a few doorbells and do some estimates and then showed me what I missed or didn't factor in. I quickly realized it was something I could do. As the summer ended, I talked to my friend and suggested we form our own painting business the following summer. He agreed, and my second business formed.

That next spring, I didn't go on a college spring break trip. Instead, I went back to Omaha and set up a painting business. I went to the local paint store and set up an account to get contractor pricing on paint and supplies. I bought some extension ladders and learned I could rent equipment like power sprayers from the paint store if that was needed for a job.

I then drove through neighborhoods, knocked on doors, and left flyers. I knocked on over 50 doors, which resulted in about 20 live conversations. I returned to school after spring break with three signed contracts. I felt pretty good about the week and was happy we had some jobs lined up for the summer.

When I ordered the paint and supplies for our first job, I told the paint store to charge my account, just like I had done at my previous company the summer before. The store owner said because I was a new account, I'd have to pay cash up front. I told him I didn't have enough to cover the paint and wouldn't be able to pay until we finished the job in a few weeks. He asked if I got any money up-front from the customer to cover my start-up costs for the job. I shook my head no. He decided I could charge it to my account, but in the future, I'd have to pay for supplies when I ordered them. I thanked him for cutting me some slack. He taught me a valuable lesson about small business cash flow challenges.

Our first job started out well, but it took us longer than anticipated to complete each step because we were only a crew of two instead of six like the previous summer. We worked harder, our breaks were shorter, and we worked many days until right before dark. I learned a valuable lesson about labor allocation and time on location. We finished our first house seven days later than our estimate, so I had to inform our other customers the start date would be delayed. Working longer hours made driving through neighborhoods for new prospects harder as well.

We got paid for our first house, and the owner even gave us a bonus for doing such a good job. What a great feeling. We deposited the check in the bank, and I went to the paint store to settle our account with the owner. Afterward, my friend and I had a celebratory beer for completing our first house as business owners. A beer never tasted so good.

Know Your Personality

I am an outgoing person, but when I recharge, I like being alone. I am right on the line between extrovert and introvert. If you don't know your personality, it can be helpful to take an online assessment to help you understand your natural wiring and how it might help or hinder your work and personal life.

In the early spring of my junior year in college, my fraternity selected candidates for rush chairman. The purpose of the job was to recruit 30 to 35 incoming freshmen to join the fraternity. I was interested and asked a close friend in my pledge class to run as co-chair. We could divide and conquer to cover more people and distance when recruiting, which required phone calls, mailed letters, and live conversations—different communication styles than today.

My rush partner and I solicited support from the other brothers in the fraternity prior to the election. We had other people running against us, so we knew we had to sway some influential chapter members if we were going to win. If elected, we'd implement a new rule that both of us had to "approve" someone getting a bid offer to join our fraternity. If we were not fully aligned, that person could not join.

On election night, we laid out our plan for rush, how we would approach it, and our plan to reach out to many of the current and former active members for potential rushees so we could put together the best class possible. It helped that I was from a larger city in the state, and my partner was from a smaller town so we could increase our reach. We won the vote that night and set out on our plan to bring in a great class of freshmen the following fall.

Our budget from the fraternity was $5,000 with the objective of bringing in 30 to 35 new recruits while filling all the remaining live-in spaces to maximize house revenue for the fall semester. It was my first lesson in setting a clear objective and measuring against that objective. In fact, it falls under the concept of S.M.A.R.T. objectives: Specific, Measurable, Achievable, Realistic, and Time-bound. This approach enables you to have a better read if you are on or off track to hit the targets you set.

Our first order of business was collaborating with active and alumni members to gather potential recruits. We received so many requests that we needed a vetting system to prioritize and focus on which candidates we personally recruited hard and those we let others in the house recruit so we could maximize our time and reach.

We looked at grades, activities, standardized test scores, any family ties back to the house, recommendations, and how they interacted with house members during social recruiting functions. We had a target list of guys we really wanted to sign, we set up social functions so recruits could get a feel for the house and current members, we solicited alumni support, and we worked the phones and hit the highways making one-on-one or small group visits to recruits' houses, sporting events, or any place where we could connect and get to know them better.

It was very similar to college sports recruiting. We tracked our budget and contacts with key people. We kept a social calendar to ensure current members could attend events and maximize the number of rushees who attended. We varied locations across the state so we could make it easier for people to attend depending on where their hometown was located.

One thing I enjoyed most was the vast number of people I met whom I would never have had the opportunity to meet otherwise. We didn't get all our top targets, but I got to know them and reconnect when I saw them on campus throughout the year.

One afternoon following a recruiting lunch a couple of hours away, I drove home in my '74 Ford Granada with the windows down and the radio turned up. I enjoyed the freedom and satisfaction of selling something I believed in and wondered if I could find something like it as a "real" job someday.

At the end of summer, we had 37 new recruits, and I had actually honed new skills. My co-chairman and I hit our objectives for the summer and returned money back to the house because we didn't spend all the budget. As the new freshmen moved into the house, it was rewarding to see them as I already had a great connection with each one of them.

Summary

As I think about my early work experiences, they were more random than planned. I see so many young people now taking a longer-term, strategic approach to their work or summer internships. I admire how they spend time at companies with future work opportunities, learn real-world skills, and create a future network of contacts. Some participate in study abroad programs that allow them to experience new working dynamics but give them a valuable lens on their world view.

It's important to reflect on what you did and what you enjoyed from your early work experiences. Many things you enjoyed back then will hold true today. I am so appreciative of those early experiences because they shaped who I am today, and also who I can become tomorrow as I continue to grow and build on those capabilities.

Chapter Questions
1. What impact in your life did early jobs have on you? What can you learn from them? How have they shaped how you think about your career or personal life?
2. If you could do any type of work, what would it be? How would it look and feel? What is preventing you from pursuing those experiences? How can you incorporate more of those activities or experiences in your life?
3. Do you have a career plan beyond the current role or work you are doing? What do the next 10 to 20 years look like for you? If you haven't written it out, I would suggest that would be a valuable use of your time. Do you have someone who is your career coach that you can seek out for advice or guidance? If not, who could help you?

Chapter 7: Lessons from Fishing

You might wonder what coaching and leadership lessons one can learn fishing from a boat in Canada. Fishing gets you to slow down and gives you time to talk and share life lessons. That is why fishing is so special to me.

My family has been going to the upper boundary waters in Ontario, Canada, for over 60 years. I have been blessed to join them for over 50 years. It's our multi-generational tradition that began with my grandfather, Norman, and has been passed down to my dad, me, and my son. My brother, Brian, joins us as well. Fishing is a passion we all share and provides experiences in which we learn from each other.

My grandfather first took my dad and his brother fishing on summer vacations. They drove on gravel roads from their home in Minnesota to remote fishing camps in the boundary waters.

My first trip to Canada was in 1972. I traveled there on a fishing trip to a fly-in camp called Zup's Fishing Lodge. We had a guide named Connie, and we slept in tents on a rocky island in the middle of a lake. I went with my grandfather, my dad, and my dad's friend, Harold.

This fishing trip was a big deal. I still remember shopping at the local sporting goods store to get fishing boots, rain gear, and a life vest. The shopping trip was a big expense for my parents, but it was a necessary part of a priceless experience for me.

Skills Passed Down

Learning usually requires someone spending time to help you learn a new skill. During my first trip, my grandfather showed me how to set up the pole and tie fishing lure knots. He was a very gentle and kind man.

The hardest part was tying the knot to ensure it was strong enough to withstand the tug and tension of a big fish on the end of the line. My first few tries were unsuccessful. It was difficult to remember how the line threaded through the loops and ended up tight and taut. I grew frustrated because I didn't want to disappoint my grandfather. He remained patient and encouraged me to keep trying, even when I failed. I finally got the hang of it and was able to assemble my fishing pole, attach my reel, and string up my line by tying knots to my lures.

Late in the week during that first trip, my dad's friend, Harold, decided to fish on his own after supper. When he returned, he had a huge walleye on his stringer and said he found a back bay where they were biting. We scrambled to get our gear and hit the spot before sundown. The good thing about fishing in Canada in the summer is it stays light late. You have good light for evening fishing, which is when walleye feed.

We pulled up into the little bay. Harold showed us the spot, and we dropped our lines in with a shiny spinner hooked with a minnow for bait. It only took 30 seconds for my dad to tie-in to a big walleye. His pole bent over the boat, and he said, "I think I caught the big one's brother."

My dad is an excellent fisherman, and he took his time with that big fish. He let that walleye sit on the bottom and tire itself out before he slowly reeled it in. He gained a couple of inches on the fish with each turn of the reel before it dove to the bottom and started all over again.

Another 15 minutes went by. The fish slowly emerged from the dark water. Harold grabbed the net as my dad brought the monster fish to the surface and toward the boat. Suddenly, it made a final dive. The reel squealed as it let out line. My dad kept working in hopes the knots he'd tied would hold and not snap the line. At last, the fish gave up and surfaced. In one swift motion, Harold scooped it out of the water and into the bottom of the boat. We all cheered before deciding it was time to head back before dark. Once back at camp, we sat around a bonfire, sharing stories from the week, and at that point, I was hooked on fishing in Canada. I've never lost my passion for it.

Brain Burners

There are some places in the world that are special to each of us, whether a few miles or thousands of miles away. I call these places "brain burners," which are places burned into your brain. You can close your eyes and put yourself there. You recall the smells, sounds, sights, and colors, and you are instantly transported there.

One of my brain burners is called Painted Rock. It's a rock that sticks out of the water on Bamaji Lake in Ontario, near Knobby's Fly-In Fishing Camp. It gets its name from the seagulls that stand on it and "paint" it while they wait for food to swim by.

Most days, Painted Rock is our last stop to fish before heading in for the night. It's also one of the best fishing spots on the entire lake. Just don't tell anyone.

But the real reason I love this spot is the great conversations and connections I have had with my family there. My first visit to the rock was as a teenager. I went through college, my early working career, getting married, losing my grandfather, having my two kids, working my way up the corporate ladder, and even missing my first fishing trip due to the global pandemic.

The beauty of the rock is it never changes. It is always present, visible, and an opportunity to connect. I have been at Painted Rock with my grandfather, and I have also had memorable conversations with my dad there. He has had meaningful conversations with my son at this part of the lake. We have been able to share the same connection, passion, and enjoyment over four generations, free from devices in the quiet of nature.

The tradition of this trip has endured because it's important to everyone. We commit to the dates and share in the work. I love Painted Rock for what it represents and for what it has given to enrich my life's experiences. Having these special places in our lives is important as they help us soak in the moment, slow down, and find joy.

Beware of the Rocks

We were in Canada one year in early fall. Birch trees had turned golden yellow, and the air was crisp with a slight chill. My dad and a few others in our group had left a day earlier, but my brother, a friend, and I stayed an extra day.

The night before the three of us were due to leave, we learned a weather front was moving in, and we might have issues leaving on time. Other than a satellite radio to contact the base camp for emergencies, there was no way to communicate with the outside world.

We woke up the next morning to rain and thunder, so we knew our floatplane out of camp would be delayed. We got our gear ready and made coffee and breakfast. The camp guide said we might be able to leave that afternoon. We fished off the shore to kill time and finally got word to take our gear to the dock.

When the floatplane arrived, the pilot urged us to load our gear as quickly as possible because the window of tolerable weather would give way to more storms behind it. We loaded our gear, boarded the plane, and fastened our seat belts. The pilot taxied to one end of the lake, revved the engine, and guided the plane off the water and into the air. I had flown this route dozens of times but never with clouds that thick or dark.

The pilot instructed us to tighten our seat belts because it was going to get bumpy. As we made our way south back to the base camp, the clouds grew thicker, rain pelted the windshield, and we flew just above the tree line to increase visibility.

I was seated in the front next to the pilot, and his expression became worried. He constantly checked his instruments while talking to base camp on his headset. Suddenly, he informed us we'd have to land on the next available lake. That wasn't a good sign.

We made a quick descent, and he instructed us to open the doors on each side of the plane while the plane was still in the air and watch for rocks below the water's surface. If we hit a rock with a pontoon while landing, it wouldn't end well. As the plane flew 80 mph, we all leaned out of our seats and scanned the water. We made it to the end of the lake, and the pilot pulled up over the treetops. We made a quick circle and headed back toward the original path.

He asked one last time if anyone had seen any rocks? We answered, "No." The pilot made his final approach. As the pontoons hit the water, we held our breath and waited, hoping not to hit any rocks. Finally, the plane slowed, and we came to a stop in the middle of the lake. He turned off the engine, and we drifted in the middle of the lake to wait out the storm.

After about an hour, the skies cleared enough to take off for base camp. We made our way down to one end of the lake, and the pilot told my brother and me to get out of the plane and stand on the pontoon, keeping an eye out for any rocks below the surface. We each stood on a pontoon, holding onto the plane with one hand, slowly moving across the lake as we watched for rocks. We did this for about 2,000 yards until the pilot told us to get back into the plane and buckle up. He asked if we saw rocks, and again, we said, "No." He turned the plane around, aimed it right back on the same path, and revved the engine. He gunned it as hard as he could. He pulled up the flaps, and we made the quickest ascent as possible with that de Havilland engine. We broke the water, rolled up into the sky, and bounced our way back to base camp.

When we landed, the camp owner asked, "How was the ride?" I looked him square in the eye and said, "Smooth sailing all the way." Then I winked because he knew what we had endured.

That experience taught me it's always better to be on the ground wishing you were in the air versus in the air wishing you were on the ground. It also reinforced that working together is the way to LIGHT up success in tough situations. One person alone would find it very challenging to dodge the storms and navigate all the rocks. It's the same way in life. Working together can help you soar safely.

Summary

No matter what your passion is, share it with others. Help them learn about those activities so they can be enjoyed across multiple generations or groups of close friends. The ability to connect, share stories, offer advice and support, and celebrate milestones across life is magical when you find it. That's something special. Never underestimate the power of time together to grow skills and learn from one another.

Chapter Questions
1. Are you finding ways to share your passions with others? What family traditions do you have or want to start that can span generations?
2. Where is your brain burner, that spot you enjoy returning to time and time again? Do you mentally go there when you need to slow down and relax?
3. What are the rocks in your life that lie below the surface? How do you look for them and navigate those challenges so you can lift off safely and soar to new heights?

Chapter 8: Mentoring

Mentoring is an important aspect in everyone's career. Early in my career, mentoring was something that happened organically. At the time, I didn't recognize it as mentoring. These mentoring relationships started and ended naturally, offering practical advice and skills that helped me throughout my career. Later, mentoring others became more of a focus of mine. I learned as much, if not more, from people I mentored as they did from me. It was definitely a mutually beneficial relationship.

Skills Mentor

One of my first mentoring relationships early in my career was with my finance manager, Mark, who supported the business for my group.

I was responsible for understanding the needs of my customers, developing programs, and designing long-term contract offers to bring back to my clients. I was good at asking the right questions to understand their needs and how my products and ideas could grow our mutual businesses. However, I needed help setting a pricing strategy to be profitable for both companies and for my personal development.

I often popped into Mark's office in the late afternoon, which was the best time for him to help me understand how pricing related to the overall profitability of each deal. He spent time explaining how one variable impacted other elements in the offer. He showed me ways to look at the deal and make it even better. We examined the length of each deal as it applied to the overall economics.

I presented my proposals to Mark so I could learn how to best position my selling story and how contract elements supported it. He offered possible customer objections and ways to navigate around them. He also explained how to make trades with the customer so we both felt like we got a good deal. Mark even shared other deals he was working on and asked me questions about how I'd structure them for maximum value.

He spent a lot of time with me, and we became close friends. By the time I left that role, I had a good understanding of profit and loss statements, as well as how the deals I proposed supported the overall direction of the company. That knowledge helped me get deals approved internally, which at times could be more challenging than getting the client to accept business terms.

That mentoring relationship set the foundation for what I was going to do later in my career. At my last assignment, I managed some of the biggest deals in our division, with hundreds of millions of dollars involved in contract agreements that spanned globally. If I had not had someone take me under their wing and shed LIGHT on areas that needed development, I would not have been able to reach those levels.

You never know what type of impact you may have on someone when you invest your time and skills in them. You have the opportunity to help them change their lives.

Development Mentor

At another role in my career, I struggled with the difference between strategy and tactics. Following conversations about a strategic customer, my mind immediately thought of tactics to add value. My manager was excellent at asking questions to test my customer knowledge and strategic thinking.

Those question-and-answer sessions used different formats. Sometimes it happened in a group setting. He'd ask us questions about our business and our customer's business. Then he'd quiz us about future opportunities for mutual growth. It was a great way to learn from peers.

Other times, small groups would go into the market and visit our customers' outlets and look for opportunities, interview staff for their insights, and shop competitive outlets to discover their best practices. Still other times, we would have top-to-top meetings with the senior leadership from the customer, review our business performance with them, and make recommendations on how we could mutually grow our collective business.

The meetings were about stewarding our business relationship and charting a path of growth for the future. I learned to always ask questions and seek out mutual growth opportunities. The key word is "mutual." Both sides need to see what's in it for them and how they win in growing the mutual business, and sometimes as important, how they win personally.

After each of these sessions, my manager asked, "As you see it now, what is your strategy with this customer?" I often listed the specific opportunities and how to capture them. He pointed out that I was confusing tactics with strategy and asked me to come back with our strategy for growth. I would leave frustrated that I couldn't clearly see the difference.

Here's the definition for each:
- Strategy defines your long-term goals and how you plan to achieve them. Your strategy gives you the path you need toward achieving your organization's mission. In other words, your strategy is how you aim to bring about a future state and the logical argument that makes it workable.
- Tactic comes from the Ancient Greek "taktikos," which loosely translates to "the art of ordering or arranging." We now use the term to denote actions or steps toward a goal. Tactics in business are short-term plans that don't deviate from the overall strategy. They include the short actions or key steps to achieve the over-arching strategy.

According to the great military strategist Sun Tzu, strategy is about winning before the battle begins, while tactics are about striking at weaknesses and building strengths during the battle.

I am a sports enthusiast, and one of my passions is college football. My manager gave me an analogy that helped bring the context of strategy and tactics into greater focus so that it finally clicked. He explained that strategy is the type of offense a team runs. The old-school Big Ten offense used a strong running game with limited passing. The West Coast offense uses mostly passing, and the Wishbone offense uses a running option game. Each of those is a strategy. However, the individual plays that are called within those offensive schemes are the tactics. You look at the defense and call the plays that capitalize on offensive strength while taking advantage of defensive weaknesses.

My job was to determine the offense I was going to install and run for my business. The tactics were the plays I was going to call to score points. His use of an analogy made perfect sense and helped me break out as a budding strategist in my career.

Again, the key element of mentoring is finding someone who will invest time in you, ask questions, create learning moments, and share their talents and experiences to help you grow on your journey. This theme of mentorship has had a profound impact on my growth and development on many fronts, not only professionally but also personally.

Mentoring Others

I wanted to find a way to give back to younger associates in my organization who had a lot of potential for business and personal growth. Several ideas were in my mind, but the one that kept bubbling back up was to form a formal career mentoring group.

I selected three people and invited my human resources business partner to be our sponsor. I reached out to each person, shared my vision for the group, and asked if they would be interested in joining. They all said yes, so in January the following year, we formed the inaugural group.

I wanted to lay out my vision for the group but also wanted my three mentees to participate in shaping the experience. The first meeting began by sharing my motivation about how other people had been instrumental in my career development, and without their help and guidance, I would not be in my current leadership role and wanted to honor them by helping others.

I invited my human resources partner to provide her expertise and then asked each person what they wanted to get out of the group. The group members said they wanted to learn from my experiences, gain clarity on their career options, and learn more about opportunities and roles in the broader organization. With those goals in mind, we identified three specific objectives for the group members:

1. Learn from my career experiences
2. Create a customized career plan for each individual
3. Explore new career options in the organization

Once we established the objectives, we set up a monthly schedule to meet and share our updates and progress. We kept each other accountable and set the agenda for the following month. Each member was 7 to 10 years into their career and had a track record of early success with business results and promotions along the way. They also had a strong desire for personal development and were in various stages of navigating their careers with marriage, family, and geographic preferences.

Their first assignment was to map out the next 25 years of their career by starting with the role they wanted before retirement and then working backward to build the skills and experiences they needed to get there. None of them had ever planned that far out. It wasn't an easy assignment. They had to sit down and do some serious self-reflection and work.

One of the results of the exercise was identifying the need to incorporate a development assignment or key area of learning for each role a person has during their career. It was the concept of "gaining two new experiences" with every role. For example, if promoted into a larger role, what other experience could you add to help you when the next opportunity presented itself?

If you have a 30-year career, you might average 10 to 12 roles during that time. If you can double each experience, you will increase your chances of going further and faster than you could without the development and growth mindset. This approach allows you to gain new experiences without having to make other personal sacrifices, such as relocating, especially as you get further in your career and more established in your life.

As the year progressed, the group worked well together. They helped and supported each other, and the program gained momentum. I wanted to expand it so more people could grow and benefit from the experience. I asked my human resources partner and other leaders in the organization for suggestions. We put a focus on female and diverse talent in the organization.

As the group expanded, my role changed. I gave them more challenging assignments that allowed them to think strategically, utilize their skills and talents, and tap into other people in the company. I was blown away by their ideas and recommendations. They formed their own sense of community, and my last assignment to them was, "How will you pay this experience forward to others?" The program worked, and we wanted to expand it even further.

The next phase was to create a larger, more official mentoring program. I asked two leaders who had a passion for coaching to create an outline for a formal mentoring program. A month later, they presented me with their plan. They wanted to match newer associates with more experienced people. They also wanted to let people self-nominate for the program, which included a survey for interests and what each person wanted to get out of the program. Based on responses, candidates would be matched and sign a formal mentoring agreement for both the mentor and mentee.

During the initial meeting with program participants, the team discussed the importance of mentoring, provided examples of positive mentoring relationships, and more importantly, they identified the "watchouts" of a mentoring pairing that doesn't work. Regular check-ins were incorporated, and the agreements included a 120-day opt-out clause for either partner if the relationship wasn't working. The formal program lasted one year, but the mentoring relationship could continue informally beyond that time frame.

The program was a great success. People who wouldn't have had the opportunity to meet connected because of the program. The formal agreement was a key element for all participants. It framed the relationship and created alignment and clarity between the partners.

Here are some of the key elements of the formal mentoring arrangement:
- Mentoring outline
- Clear roles for the mentor and mentee
- 2 to 3 objectives that can be defined by both parties
- Clearly defined frequency for the meetings
- Clarity on who sets the agenda topics
- Duration of the mentoring agreement (usually one year)
- 120-day no-fault termination if the mentoring relationship isn't working for either party
- Ability to extend if both parties mutually agree

Formalizing these points into a written agreement and having both parties sign off on the mentoring plan ensures alignment. It helps clarify the relationship and sets appropriate expectations and boundaries for all parties.

Summary

Mentoring is an important developmental tool for everyone in their careers and lives. It's natural that earlier in life, you may be mentored more, but that doesn't mean you can't contribute or add to the mentoring relationship. Being open to having others help and guide you is an important mindset. No one has things completely figured out.

Take the time to listen and learn. You will be amazed at where it can take you in life.

I am so grateful for the incredible mentors in my life. I would not be the person I am without their belief, time, and investment in me. Make sure you are creating your legacy of mentoring and helping others. You never know when and how you can change someone else's life for the better.

Chapter Questions
1. Who have been some of your most important mentors? What have they contributed to your growth and development? Do they know the impact they have had on you? If not, reach out to them and let them know.
2. How are you mentoring others? Are you making the investment of time to help someone else? If not, what is getting in your way? Your belief in someone else is a force multiplier in their life.
3. What do you know now that you wished you knew earlier in your career? How can you share that with others? Sharing your story is a powerful way to help and mentor others.

Chapter 9: Setbacks

I have had many setbacks and failures in my life. When they happen, they are not enjoyable. I often think about how they can be avoided or minimized. Who wants to feel like you aren't good enough or capable? Not me, but as I reflect on them, they are necessary and need to be embraced for the growth opportunity they present.

Embracing failure is counterintuitive. In my mind, failure should be avoided. But failure sets you up for future success; you just don't know it yet. You have to grow and learn from it. How many times in your life have you been successful at something from the start? For me, not many.

Successful Rebounding

When I was in high school, a state basketball All-Star team was selected each year to participate in a summer tournament in Las Vegas. Each participating state held tryouts and selected players for the tournament.

Each year I followed the progress of the players selected from my state and reviewed the game statistics. I set my sights on earning a spot on that team the summer before my senior year. High school coaches nominated players to try out.

I received a letter in the mail and was invited to try out for the team in Lincoln, Nebraska, at a local college. I knew I had a chance to make the team, but it wasn't a given.

My dad drove me to Lincoln, and as I got out of the car, he told me to do my best and have fun. His words of encouragement meant a lot to me.

I checked in at the main table, was handed a pullover jersey, and told to practice shooting until tryouts started. I knew most of the local players in my city, but others were new faces. We sized each other up and pretended tryouts weren't a big deal, but they were.

About five head coaches from around the state made up the staff and selection committee. It was a mix of small and large high schools from around the state. They divided us into groups for basic drills. It was important to hit your shot, play sound defense, and hustle in every drill.

I felt pretty good about how things started. I was in my groove, and my shot was on. Next, we were grouped into teams of 7 to 8 players for a live scrimmage. They would periodically mix up the teams to determine how different players worked together. I kept changing teams, making it difficult to get into a rhythm with a group, and I knew I was in the lower rung of players. I put that out of my mind and focused on what I could control.

I played my best defense and made sharp passes, but my shot was not where it needed to be. In hindsight, I forced some shots to get noticed instead of playing my game.

As the scrimmage ended, they pulled us all into the center of the main court and said we'd receive a call by the following week to notify us whether we made the team or not. I thought I played well enough to make the team but knew it was going to be close. I hoped to make it because I got to know some of the guys and wanted to continue with the team.

The following week the phone rang during supper. I answered, knowing it could be the call I was anticipating. My heart raced. It was one of the coaches from tryouts. He said I played well but didn't make the team. He wished me the best and said he'd look forward to following my senior basketball season.

My family knew by the conversation that I had not made the team. My dad told me to focus on getting better over the summer and have a great senior year. My mom told me she loved me and was proud of me.

I was devastated! That night I cried with disappointment. The next morning, I woke up, put on my basketball shoes, and went out to the driveway to start practicing for my senior year. There was no sense in feeling sorry for myself. It was time to do something about it and get better.

I worked hard that summer. I honed my shooting skills. I improved my ability to drive to the hoop and make the shot after someone made contact with me to create more scoring opportunities. I also worked on my defense during summer camps and summer league games.

I had a very good senior year. I was a captain on the team and led in scoring. Even though I took a few recruiting trips to Division II schools, I knew in my heart that my basketball career was coming to an end. I had some issues with my knees and didn't want to spend my college years nursing an injury.

I played my last competitive game in our district's final my senior year. We didn't win or make it to the state tournament that year, but I had the best and most enjoyable year of my high school career.

Playing basketball taught me many positive life lessons that are still valuable to me today: hard work, being a good teammate, being coachable, remaining calm under pressure, and being a leader on and off the court.

Burn the Ribs

My father-in-law, Paul Wade, recently passed away at the age of 81. He was a good man. He was fun-loving and enjoyed a cold beer while tending to the BBQ.

In my mid-20s, I had recently become engaged to his only daughter, Alisa, and we were on his back deck over a Memorial Day weekend. Paul wanted to try something new and smoke some St. Louis-style baby back ribs for dinner. I was new to using a smoker, so I looked forward to learning about it. I grew up watching my dad grill steaks on charcoal, but we didn't cook meat on a smoker.

It was a bright and sunny summer day with a gentle breeze. We prepared the ribs and put them on the smoker. The smell of hickory filled the backyard. The Indianapolis 500 car race was on, so we pulled the TV to the back deck and placed it in a shady corner. We talked about life, had some cold beers, and enjoyed the afternoon.

Paul asked when to put the BBQ sauce on the ribs. I really didn't know but figured the sauce could marinate the meat to give it more flavor. We lathered on the sauce and set the lid back on the smoker, letting the ribs cook another three hours.

A little before dinner time, Alisa and her Mom returned from wedding shopping. I helped set the table, and Paul asked me to pull the ribs off the smoker and bring them inside. I grabbed a platter, found the tongs, and went back out to the deck. I opened the smoker lid and stared at the ribs. They were burnt to a crisp. They were charred and had a thick black crust. I was so disappointed. I put them on the platter and hoped they'd still taste okay.

I tried one, and it tasted like it looked. The rib was crusty, dry, and had a burned taste on the outside. The sugar in the sauce burned and charred from being left on too long. I called Paul over for his opinion. He took a bite and said, "Looks like we are having pizza tonight." We ordered pizza and had it with our potato salad and baked beans.

Over the years, Paul and I kept trying to perfect our BBQ rib recipes. We tried boiling the ribs and then smoking them. We tried smoking them and then finishing them in the oven. We used a kettle BBQ without any sauce.

After years and years of trying, we finally found a process and recipe that worked every time. Like any good BBQ enthusiast, I can't tell you how we smoke our ribs. It's a family secret.

The best part about burning the ribs our first time is that every time after that was always going to be better than our first try. Paul and I enjoyed the process of learning how to cook perfect ribs. We asked all kinds of people how they cooked ribs and shared what we learned with each other. We tried new techniques and processes, retaining some aspects and discarding others. For us, it was about the journey of learning and sharing.

I learned a similar lesson in business from a high-ranking leader. He said, "John, make your first meeting with a client your worst meeting." At first, it didn't make sense to me. He explained that it was important to get all the issues on the table for both sides, air the grievances, and then create a joint plan to make the partnership better. In other words, it's better to burn the ribs in the beginning and commit to making them better over time. What a powerful lesson in life and business.

Timing Is Everything

Sometimes you need a combination of luck and divine intervention to work at one company for over 32 years in corporate America. Timing is also critical, and it helps to get advice at just the right time so that things go in your favor. But the real key is asking yourself what is driving the behavior in the first place. Shining LIGHT on that aspect will allow for growth and success from the advice you receive.

I had been in my first role right out of college for about a year. I was figuring out the job and settled into a good routine in my business. I was in an entry-level sales position calling on local mom-and-pop restaurants.

I enjoyed interacting with the customers. I met all kinds of people, and I loved hearing the stories about how they got into the restaurant business. Some had been in the industry for many generations, and others were transitioning from different careers to fulfill a dream. Restaurant owners have a hospitality mindset, which usually comes through in everything they do.

However, I didn't enjoy the daily and weekly administrative activities of the job. All the forms, approvals, and processes got in the way of getting out in my territory and spending more time with existing and potential new customers.

True salespeople prefer to be out selling. The more you put on their plate to facilitate the sale after the fact, the less fulfilling it becomes. If you ask a salesperson to do things that are not in front of a customer selling, then you reduce your revenue opportunity and crush a true salesperson's soul. If you ask them to collect payments from customers who are overdue, you risk them losing sight of what drives top-line revenue for your business.

This happened to me early in my career, and I started to look at different jobs outside of my company. For weeks I scanned the jobs section of the newspaper until a listing finally caught my eye. It was marketed as an entrepreneurial opportunity to own your own business and create passive income by others selling underneath you. The product was fire extinguishers, which was a big departure from selling for a Fortune 100 company, but the focus on selling without a lot of process appealed to me at the time.

I mailed my resume to the recruiter and eventually met with him at a little office. He had all the charts and projections showing what I could make depending on how many fire extinguishers my network and I could sell per month. The more people I brought in underneath me, the more potential income I could generate. I thought I could easily double my salary.

He said a lot of people wanted the position, so I needed to secure it with a $100 deposit. I didn't always have an extra $100 in my checking account, so it was good I had just been paid. I decided to go for it and chart my own destiny in the fire extinguisher business. I wrote my check and planned to let my boss know I was moving on to greener pastures. I didn't realize I was giving up an amazing job with a great company to enter a Ponzi scheme.

I met my girlfriend (now wife) for lunch to share the exciting news. I arrived at the restaurant a little early and decided to call my boss and quit. I found a payphone and dialed. The call rolled to voicemail, which meant our office assistant was at lunch. I hung up and decided to call again after lunch. It turned out to be one of the most fortunate calls that went unanswered in my entire life.

My girlfriend arrived, and I told her I had some exciting news. She knew I wasn't happy at my current job and was looking at other opportunities. I told her I was starting my own business selling fire extinguishers. Her mouth fell open in disbelief. She asked if I had lost my mind. Then she told me to call the bank and cancel the $100 check, which I did.

After that call, we talked about why I wanted to make the change. She asked if I had discussed my concerns with my manager, which I hadn't. She suggested I schedule time with my manager to better understand what was required and what was nice to do but not always mandatory. It made sense, so I agreed to give my current job a little longer to see if things improved.

My wife worked in human resources later in her career, and I always told her she had plenty of training from all the coaching she gave me over the years.

I received a phone call after lunch from the fire extinguisher recruiter, asking why I canceled the check. I told him I had a change of heart and was going to keep my current job. He told me I was missing out on an amazing opportunity. The actual amazing opportunity ended up being my 32-year career with one company. I will always cherish the people I met and the opportunities for growth that I was able to experience. I owe that and a lot of other amazing things to my beautiful wife, Alisa. She is always there to give me the advice I need to hear.

Summary

You need to experience setbacks in your life to give you perspective on how to adapt and change to move forward. It's never easy to embrace failures or challenges, but they help make you who you are today and who you will be in the future.

If something is difficult, sit back and ask why it's difficult and what you can learn from it. Don't blame outside factors for your failures. Unfair circumstances or a bad boss may be contributors, but you need to examine the role you played.

I contributed to my unhappiness in my job by not reaching out to my boss to discuss the challenges I was having. I thought the only solution was to quit, but that was only one solution. By having the courage to openly share my challenges, I created more opportunities for growth.

I got lucky my boss didn't answer the phone that day, but don't leave big decisions up to luck. Let people know how you are doing and create a plan together in both your professional and personal life.

Chapter Questions
1. What are some of your biggest failures in life? How have you responded to them? How did they shape or change your life? How did you grow?
2. What is a passion in your life? How have you made mistakes or failed in the pursuit of your passion? Could you be where you are now with your passion if you hadn't taken some chances, failed, and then learned something new to grow?
3. If you are struggling, who can you reach out to for advice? Tell a boss, a coach, or a friend where you stand and where you need help. You will be amazed at how good it feels and how much they can help you consider your options. When life gets difficult, keep shining LIGHT on your path. Asking for help is a sign of strength, not weakness.

L
I
G
Healthy Relationships Matter
T

Chapter 10: Less Boozing, More Moving

Early in my career, I enjoyed meeting coworkers for social gatherings. We played in company-sponsored sports leagues like softball and kickball. These events were a great way to create bonds and friendships with people at work. Spouses or significant others played as well. After the games, we headed to a local sports bar to have pizza, burgers, and beer. We talked about the game and life in general.

Socializing outside the office had positive benefits as it deepened your understanding of a person and brought you closer together. We had many positive outings, but I also witnessed some negative encounters.

Drinking at work functions can be a trap. Maybe not for everyone, but it is for some. The bar acts like your friend, but it isn't. Most social work functions begin in a similar manner. Coworkers want to get to know each other; they have good intentions. People are chatting and buying each other drinks. Before you know it, someone has had a few too many.

The Bar Is Not Your Friend

As a rule, you should never have more than two drinks at a work event. Nobody has ever said they "didn't drink enough" or "went to bed too early" the morning following a social function for work. Instead, coworkers gossip about what someone said or did at the event or make note of who came to work late because they overslept or were hungover.

If you are a new professional or new to leading people, you need to be aware of these situations. Just because you're at a bar doesn't mean it's not a work function. You can still socialize, but don't forget the context in which you're operating.

As a leader, I had to be on call with a clear mind 24/7. Sometimes my cell phone rang in the middle of the night, and it was my counterpart from human resources. Those calls were stressful because I knew something had happened that put someone's safety or career in danger. I had to uphold the company's rules and policies governing these matters and handle the situation with clear faculties.

One time, it was about two o'clock in the morning on day two of a regional company meeting. My phone rang in the middle of the night, startling me out of a deep sleep. My human resources partner said, "John, we have a situation, and I need your help."

I got dressed, splashed some water on my face, put on my baseball cap, and headed down to the hotel lobby. I got an overview of the situation, and it wasn't good. Someone had gotten drunk, behaved inappropriately to another employee, and then passed out in the hotel. I knew the person who had gotten drunk, and my first reaction was to feel bad for them. But as a leader, I had to act.

My primary concern was for the person who was treated unfairly and disrespected. Core values must always come first. My second concern was for the individual who got drunk because clearly, something was not right in their life. I asked my human resources business partner for an internal investigation to sort out the situation. This was their area of expertise.

The full report came back with a range of disciplinary options. Given the severity of the behavior, this person was terminated from the company.

Not all situations end this way but don't let alcohol or drugs impact your reputation or career opportunities. As a leader, set up social events that don't promote situations where people can get into trouble. Every individual is responsible for their own behavior, but I have seen some situations that can lead to more issues than necessary.

I learned later in my career that people don't care if you are drinking alcohol or something non-alcoholic. They just want to socialize and enjoy. My go-to drink of choice at business functions was a club soda with lime. If someone offered me something alcoholic, I would say, "I am good with what I have," and nobody cared. This choice also allowed me to be clear and ready to act if needed.

Examine your personal boundaries or strategies for company social functions. If you are going to drink alcohol, have a plan in advance and stick to it. You will be better off the next morning, and your career will thank you for it.

The Scale Doesn't Lie

In the middle of my career, I started a role that required me to travel almost every week of the year. I lived in Denver, Colorado, and I had responsibility for a sales organization in 14 states across the Western US. Most weeks, I flew to two or three cities per week. My days were filled with customer meetings or internal team meetings and evenings with long client dinners.

I was focused on my team and adding value for my company, so when I got back home, I could devote more time to family activities. My wife and I enjoyed taking car rides to see the beauty of Colorado. I also enjoyed a round of golf with my buddies on a Saturday when I could get away. However, I was neglecting one important thing—my health.

Every year before the holidays, I weighed myself. The rest of the year, I judged my weight and health by how my clothes fit. Each year I gained about five pounds but promised to start working out and eating healthier after the holidays. It never happened.

After the fifth consecutive year, I realized my health was going to go one of two ways: either I'd be unhealthy, or I'd make some real changes. On one of my last flights of the year, I overheard the person sitting next to me complaining about the size of the person next to him. He was talking about me!

It upset me, but deep down, I knew he was right. His conversation was a gift. It was the motivation I needed to make long-term changes. And it started with simply moving more. I was going to run, walk, and do whatever else was needed to get me to move more five days per week.

For the first business trip I took after the holidays, I packed my tennis shoes, workout clothes, and a motivational music playlist. I designated it my "move more" program.

The hotel I stayed at was like a second home. When I arrived, I went to my room, put on my workout gear, and sat on the bed. I realized I didn't know where the hotel gym was located. I got on the elevator, went to the front desk, and asked where I could access the gym. The nice person at the front desk told me to go to the second floor, and the gym would be on the right when I got off the elevators. I had walked by that door many times over the previous few years, and I never knew there was a gym there.

During that trip, I discovered if I worked out early in the morning, my success rate was higher than if I tried to work out in the evening. I made it a priority to do this first thing after I woke up. At first, it was difficult. Then it became easier and easier. I was making this a part of my regular weekly routine and actually started looking forward to it each day.

My first time staying in Las Vegas was an eye-opening experience with my new "move more" program. I had my typical schedule of meetings and dinners but still packed my workout gear. I woke up and headed downstairs to get a workout in the hotel gym. The elevator door opened to the casino floor. It was 6 am, but the slot machines dinged, and cigarette smoke filled the casino as I made my way to the gym. Of everyone on the casino floor, I was the only one wearing workout clothes.

I reached the gym, which had some of the best exercise equipment I had seen. It was almost empty. I put in my earbuds, cranked up some music, and started my "Vegas workout."

As I left the gym, I had a great, natural high and a renewed confidence in myself that this was going to work. I felt better, my outlook on life was more positive, and I knew things were going in the right direction.

My wife and I enjoyed more walks and hikes in the foothills of Colorado, and this entirely new world opened.

In December of that year, I did my pre-holiday weigh-in. I stepped on the scale. The digital numbers popped up. There it was. I had lost 30 pounds in the last 12 months. It felt great! It also motivated me to keep moving over the holidays so I didn't lose ground on my success.

In the next 24 months, I lost another 20 pounds and have kept it off for the past five years. You need to make your health a priority because without it, nothing else matters.

Summary

Health and wellbeing are important themes in my life. I have had experiences when it was in balance and other times when it was out of balance. Knowing where you are in your health journey is very important. How you show up in your life matters. You are responsible for your behavior and its results. Make sure you have a plan to protect your health, overall wellbeing, and relationships.

When something is not going the way you want, stop for a personal time out and reflection. What is causing it? What is preventing you from changing it? Be honest with yourself. If you cannot find the solution on your own, don't be afraid to ask for help. Sometimes you just need another perspective. You can never take your reputation or health for granted. A healthy relationship with yourself matters!

Chapter Questions
1. What strategies do you have to set boundaries at work functions? What outcomes have you seen as a result?
2. What are the things in your life that you want to change or improve? What obstacles are in your way? Shine a LIGHT on what is getting in your way. The longer you wait, the more difficult it will become to change. Focus on your goal and take small steps. Over time small steps lead to significant progress.
3. Do you have someone who can serve as an accountability coach to help keep you on track with your goals? This concept has been a big help to me in writing this book. Give it a try. It worked for me.

Chapter 11: Coach's Tips

One of the questions I would often hear later in my career was, "What do you know now that you wish you knew early in your career?" One of my answers was I wished I would have slowed down more, both in my professional and personal life.

I was always in a hurry to accomplish the next deal. I was in a hurry to get the next promotion. I was in a hurry to get to the next city for a customer meeting. I was in a hurry for the weekend to come.

I wish I had slowed down more and enjoyed the ride. I wish I had been more present in my children's lives. I wish I had learned earlier that it wasn't about me as a leader. It was about the people for whom I was responsible.

I still struggle with slowing down, but I am a work in progress and getting much more intentional about it each and every day. The following sections cover some tips for focusing on your relationship with others and slowing down to make better decisions.

What Are You Working On, and How Can I Help?

For most of my time as a leader, I wanted to understand how my team was doing in pursuit of our team goals. But often, I wasn't really focused on the team's goal. I was focused on my goal and the number I was responsible for delivering to my manager. I wanted status updates on how they were delivering on their goals. Did they think they were going to be on plan, over plan, or worse yet, below plan?

I was too focused on the goals and not focused on how people were doing or what help they needed from me to be successful. During meetings, I peppered them with questions and reminded them they were accountable for the numbers that most of the time they didn't even set. It was very much a top-down annual planning process. Everyone knew it was an exercise to get to a revenue target even if it was positioned as a bottom-up, opportunity-based planning process to hit a predetermined target.

The next time you sit down to have a "check-in," "one-on-one," "monthly review," or whatever else you call a meeting between a manager and associate, ask this question, "What are you working on and how can I help?" You can close the meeting by asking, "Do you have the tools and resources to be successful?" This will turn the meeting from being about you as a leader and put the focus on helping the people you lead or influence. The results will follow when you change your focus.

You Only Need to Be Right at the End of the Meeting

I worked at the same company and in the same division for my entire 32-year career. I observed similar opportunities and challenges for decades that would form my point of view on many topics. This could be a strength and, at the same time, a weakness.

Many things in our experiences and personal wiring can be this "Yin & Yang" in life. If I walked into a meeting and knew the agenda items, I had a strong point of view on how to accelerate an opportunity or handle an issue or challenge. I relied on facts or data that supported my point and discounted or ignored points that were counter to my belief. This didn't happen all the time but more often than I realized.

Then, an instructor of a training class said our job as a leader wasn't to be right at the beginning of the meeting. Our job was to be right at the end of the meeting.

That concept completely changed how I approached meetings going forward. It forced me to slow down. I didn't have to rush to a decision. I asked more questions and engaged others for their points of view. I asked if this was their decision, what would they do and why? Even though I still had strong opinions going into the meetings, I remained open to other ideas and possibilities and often found a new alternative by combining ideas or strategies that built off the collective genius of the group.

If you find as a leader that you are making the final decisions and don't change your perspective, you are missing out on the talent and experience of the group. Be right, but it's necessary only at the end of meetings when decisions need to be made.

A Slow 'Yes' Is Better than a Fast 'No'

In my later roles, I had many people in my organization looking for approval to advance an idea or deal. Sometimes they were on a deadline to meet an internal or external request. When they would pitch it to me, I always asked when they needed my decision. If they wanted approval on the spot but did not have a truly pressing deadline, I asked, "Do you want a fast no or a slower yes?"

Many times, I asked for more information or for others to weigh in or re-work certain sections of the idea or proposal to make it better. If you gain buy-in over time with stakeholders, your chances for approval go up significantly, and your ideas are better thought out. You may even change your ideas based on other people's experiences and perspectives.

Those relationships will make your decision better. By not making recommendations in a vacuum, you find areas that need to be addressed. I preferred it when someone asked me for feedback, sought further input and improvement from others, and then returned with a final product that had been enhanced with multiple points of view. It takes longer, is more involved, and slows down the process, but in the end, the idea or product is usually better.

Stay In the Pocket More

I enjoy sports analogies. As a kid, we played whatever sport was in season: football in the fall, baseball in the summer, and basketball in the winter. One of our favorite games was to re-create iconic plays by college or professional athletes in the backyard. We pretended to be a great wide receiver going up for a game-winning touchdown. We counted down the end of the basketball game and took the winning shot to see it swish through the net. Often, we dropped the winning touchdown pass or hit the back of the rim and did not make the winning play. However, the beauty of backyard sports is you could keep trying until you made the play before you went home for the night.

I get excited about new projects, ideas, and activities. I dive into them with passion and excitement. Slowing down in that moment can be challenging. However, when I temper that excitement, I connect better with others, am more aware, and make better decisions.

One of my favorite sayings is, "Stay in the pocket longer." I love football, and arguably the most important position on the team is the quarterback. They can see the entire field, they don't force passes into tight coverage, and they know when to throw the ball away and wait for a better play. An experienced quarterback can stay in the pocket and wait to throw the ball to a receiver until the last second before the defense tackles them. That patience and timing can lead to making a better play.

Taking your time, not locking into one receiver, and looking at other options that may lead to a better play are all concepts that apply in life. On the other hand, a less experienced quarterback will rush plays. An inexperienced quarterback knows the play but follows their primary receiver until they feel the defense closing in, and then they throw the ball to that receiver, even if that receiver isn't open. An experienced defender will observe this tendency and exploit it. They will follow the quarterback's head to identify the intended receiver, then intercept the pass or break it up for an incompletion.

The same is true in life. Don't lock into one approach. Let people around you help you make better decisions based on their skills or experiences.

When I stay open, exercise patience, and let the decision play out, I make better decisions. A good example of this was when my wife and I went shopping for a new vehicle. We knew the brand we wanted, which had two different styles. We figured after a test drive of each style, we'd decide and drive it off the lot that afternoon.

We walked into the dealership and found a salesperson to help us. My wife test drove her preferred style while I rode in the back. I really liked the size, ride, and features.

Next, I drove the style I preferred. It had a bigger engine, more room, and I was more comfortable in it. I loved it!

We got back to the dealership and went into the salesperson's office to discuss our decision. My wife loved her style, and I loved mine. We were at an impasse, and my wife and I knew we weren't ready to decide. We wanted to take our time, think about it, and keep looking for more options.

We waited another six weeks, looked at more vehicles, and went to another dealer. We test drove a different vehicle, and we both loved it. It was an easy decision for both of us. We bought the car on the spot. We stayed in the pocket until a better option came our way.

What Else?

Nobody likes a meeting that runs long and drags on with no end in sight. It's important to have a clear agenda and understand why each person is being invited to the meeting. It's also important to have a clear understanding of the decisions made and the next steps at the end of a meeting.

I picked up a tip a few years ago called, "What else?" It's a way to engage people during meetings and truly give everyone a chance to participate. Maybe someone has an idea or suggestion but doesn't feel comfortable sharing it with the group. Maybe someone in the meeting is taking up a lot of time making their point or grandstanding in front of the leader. Maybe a person is new and doesn't feel secure contributing yet. Asking the question, "What else?" gives everyone an invitation to share.

I didn't think it would make a lot of difference until I started to implement the concept. You need to plan if you're going to implement the idea. If you wait until the very end of the meeting to ask the question, you will run out of time.

Ask with at least 15 minutes left in the meeting, "Before we conclude, what else is out there that we should consider or think about?" Be prepared for dead silence. That's okay. Just let the question sit. It will feel very uncomfortable, but someone will have something to add—I promise. And when it happens, stay open to it. Let others contribute. This might be the moment someone has been waiting for since the meeting started. Encourage others to build on or add.

I have seen some of the best ideas come out of this technique. You are building an environment where others can have their voices heard, and it gives you additional ideas to consider. Plan for it and take note of the ideas that come from the final minutes of the meeting. It's worth its weight in gold.

Feedback Is a Gift

Often in my career, I heard that feedback is a gift. Early on, my managers asked if I was open to feedback. I took it as code for, "Let me tell you where you didn't measure up to expectations, and then let me know how you are going to improve." It was often during the annual review process, which felt forced because it was a requirement.

If it was the first time I heard the feedback regarding something that had happened months prior, I felt frustrated. I would prefer to hear the feedback in real-time. That allowed me to consider the feedback and make the necessary changes in real-time.

When I became a leader, I wanted to let people know how they were doing more in the moment versus waiting until the annual review cycle. That feedback can be about what needs to be improved but also what they are doing well. Both are helpful and shine LIGHT on the path to more success.

My early view on feedback was driven by my own uncertainty regarding my performance and lack of confidence in my abilities.

A confident individual takes feedback for what it is. Feedback is an opportunity for growth and improvement if you are open to it. It is also a sign of a healthy relationship. As I progressed in my career and had more success, I became much more open to it and actively sought out feedback. The real irony is as you move up to roles of increasing responsibility, you get less feedback even though it can be even more impactful given the size and scale of the business you are leading.

Many times, you get feedback from people who are trying to gain your favor instead of giving an honest assessment of your performance. Be aware of motivation. Don't dismiss critical feedback because you think somebody doesn't like you or doesn't understand how things really are. Slow down and ask questions regarding what success looks like to them or ask them to explain their feedback in more detail. If you embrace the exchange, you will improve because of that relationship and advice.

It is healthy to have people challenge you and encourage you to do some introspection. Only disregard the feedback if you are satisfied with how things are going and don't have a desire to improve.

Summary

It is important to turn the conversation around and make it about others and how you as a leader can support them. Once you make that mental shift, you go from a boss to a servant leader who is more concerned about your team and the broader organization. You will be a better coach and leader who supports people along their journey.

Set clear objectives knowing you will not have to be solely responsible for achieving the result. I wish I had learned this much earlier in my career. Remember to slow down when making a big decision. It doesn't always seem like what you should do in the moment, but by slowing down, you will make a better and more well-informed decision. Slowing down also lets you go faster over time. It will help you and others, and it will lead to stronger, healthier relationships.

Chapter Questions

1. Are you currently struggling with a decision? Why? Who can you seek out for advice and counsel? Keep asking why until you uncover the root cause and then work that angle. In the end, it will be a better decision. Stay in the pocket.
2. How are you gaining input from all voices on your team? How can you engage more people? Ask your team members how you can improve meetings or interactions, then be open to making that change happen.
3. When you have a one-on-one conversation with someone, who talks the most? If you, as the leader, talk more, then you aren't listening and learning how you can support that person and help them grow. It's not about you. It's about them. Next time, ask how they are doing and where they might need your help or support. Observe how that shift works for you as a leader.
4. Do you find yourself anchoring hard on your point of view during a meeting? If so, relax. You only have to be right at the end. Be open to new ideas and approaches. You don't have to have all the answers. If you do, then you need a new team.
5. When was the last time you received difficult feedback? What was your reaction? What did you learn about yourself? Did you do anything differently going forward?

LIGHT
Take Your Shot

Chapter 12: Keep Taking Your Shot

Nothing goes perfectly all the time. But just because something isn't going the way you want doesn't mean you should give up. Trust your training, believe in your instincts, and listen to your coaches.

Try and Try Again

I was a senior in high school, and it was a cold January night as I departed the old, yellow school bus for our basketball game. The wind whipped, and the cold snow crunched under my feet. I felt the excitement as my team made its way toward the gymnasium.

I knew it was going to be a special night. We were playing our high school basketball rival, and we were the only game in town that Wednesday night. During warm-ups, the band played, the cheerleaders performed, and the crowd buzzed with excitement.

In the locker room, our coach gave us one last set of instructions related to defense and our first couple of plays on offense. He let us know we controlled our effort and to leave it on the court. I led the team in our pre-game prayer as I did all of my senior year. I asked for strength and guidance. We had a moment of silence and then headed down the hallway and into the bright lights of the gymnasium. Everything was illuminated and clear as I had been practicing for this night my entire life.

I looked up into the crowd and saw my parents in the stands, sitting with the rest of the team's fans. It was nice to know they were there cheering us on. The band played "On Broadway" by George Benson, a common song played at many high school games in the 80s.

The game started out as expected—tough-nosed defense, no easy shots, and intensity on both ends of the court. I had a few open looks early in the game but couldn't get it going offensively. Every time I got over the half-court line, a defender met me and didn't give me any room to get open. I made a few moves to the hoop, but then another defensive player dropped off to double-team me. We stayed in the game in the first half, but we were losing at halftime by five points. I wasn't much of an offensive factor, going 2-7 with only four points to show for my efforts.

We gathered in the locker room at halftime, and Coach told us to settle down and play our game. We were still in it and didn't play our best in the first half. He broke down the opponent's defense, and he had offensive plays for us to run in response. Our coach was good at making concepts easy for everyone on the team to understand. His instructions were clear and crisp. He had everyone's attention in the locker room.

We had a good plan for the second half. Before leaving the locker room, our coach asked me to come over to him for some final instructions. He looked at me straight in the eye and said, "John, if we are going to win, you have to keep taking your shot."

I looked right back at him and said, "I will."

The second half started off with the same intensity, but the rim seemed bigger, and my game was flowing. My shot started to pick up. I was a streak shooter. When I found my rhythm, the game came easier for me. My confidence increased, and my overall game improved with it.

Confidence is such a big factor in anything we take on. When the other team guarded me with two players, I found an open teammate for an easy shot. My step to the basket was quicker, and my opponent tired. I was also making free throws down the stretch. The other team grew desperate, but they never gave up. It was close to the end.

The buzzer sounded, and we won by four points. Our coach gave me a big bear hug and said, "I knew you had it in you if you just trusted yourself to keep taking your shot." Sometimes you just need a coach to see something in you even if you don't see it in yourself. A strong relationship with a coach can make such a big impact.

Whatever you choose to do with your professional career, sharpen your skills with confidence, listen to your coach, trust yourself, and keep taking your shot to succeed.

Compassion Is Key

Early in my professional career as a new salesperson, I attended a three-day training course on how to sell in a consistent, professional manner. Thirty new hires attended the training to obtain selling credentials, learn processes, and master the language.

The training curriculum included small break-out sessions for learning, role-playing, and obtaining instant feedback from the instructor. The concepts made sense, and I quickly determined how to apply them to the small Midwest restaurants I sold to in my territory.

On the second day of training, it was my turn to role play a specific concept. We used questions to uncover opportunities for our solutions that were helpful to a local restaurant concept. I opened the conversation well, but toward the middle, my questions were too vague, and they didn't get to the opportunities fast enough. I struggled, and the role-playing didn't go well. The instructor's feedback was harsh and blunt, and I doubted I'd be able to put the concept to use in the field. I left that session feeling pretty down.

A colleague and friend performed the role play in the next training session. This time, the senior vice president of the program joined the instructor, which raised the intensity in the room. This senior vice president influenced future opportunities and promotions, so it was like having another job interview.

My colleague and I teamed up. He led the role play, and I was the customer. He had a strong opening. Then his expression shifted, and I knew he was unsure how to transition into framing the opportunity. My heart sank. He resorted to humor to get back on track. It was awkward, but people chuckled, and it got him back in the flow. He ended the session on a strong note with a solid closing comment and tangible next steps, just like the training outlined.

The instructor pointed out his inconsistencies according to the training. He criticized the use of humor as being unprofessional and undermining his credibility. What came next is a true sign of leadership. The vice president weighed in, saying that although my colleague didn't follow the training outline, humor can be appropriate because it provides an opportunity to change the conversation and break the ice when a situation is tense. That comment changed the entire mood of the room.

Another class participant shared how humor helped them with their openings, especially early on in a sales call when it is challenging to find common ground. The instructor didn't seem to be offended, in part because the vice president acknowledged that his feedback was accurate.

The exchange demonstrated that a narrow view can be limiting, and looking for the good in someone's approach can provide encouragement and allow constructive feedback to better sink in.

That leadership lesson has stuck with me for over 25 years. I realized you need to give direct feedback to people in a way that is clear and compassionate. You don't need to tear the person down to make your point. You can understand and empathize with their challenges and guide them to a more effective option. People need to be able to follow the training but do it in their own style for it to be authentic. One style does not fit everyone.

Be a Leader of Leaders

Later in my career, I had multiple levels of leaders with hundreds of people in my organization. This transition required a new set of skills and strategies. I received a promotion to the vice president position that covered the western US based in Denver, Colorado. In this role, my direct reports were all directors of sales, and they each had their own sales teams. I had just been promoted from a director of sales position myself, so I knew a lot about their jobs. That turned out to be both good and bad at times.

One of the first things I wanted to do in my new role was to get to know my new directors and their teams. I set up a trip to the Pacific Northwest to meet with my director in that territory and some of her team members. I had a one-on-one with her and shared my leadership philosophy. I learned how she wanted to work with me. She said she knew her team and customers, and when she needed some help and guidance, she would reach out and let me know. I thought that sounded reasonable and assured her I would support her and her team. We then went into the market to visit some locations and meet her team to better understand the business in this area.

As we met with the team members, I was excited to be in my new role and wanted to share with them the things I saw as opportunities for growth in the business. I also asked what her team members saw as opportunities and made sure they followed up with me on their progress. I thought we had a very insightful and engaging day in the field. As we were finishing up, my director asked if we could sit down and review our day together.

I thought it was a good idea to ensure we had a good follow-up routine so we could track progress. She said, "John, I am so glad you are in your role because you are going to make my job very easy." I thought it was a nice compliment, and I felt good that I had added value from the start.

She went on to say, "If you are going to lead my team like you are their boss, then you won't need me." Suddenly, I was confused. She continued, "You need to make a decision. Are you going to be the director and lead my team, or will you be the vice president and lead me and my peers? It's your choice, but let me know which one you choose." She got up, packed her things, and left.

I had some thinking to do on how I was going to approach my new role. I needed to better understand when it was my shot to take and when I should pass the ball.

On the flight home that night, I decided to change my perspective on what leading leaders was all about and how I was going to support my organization. I wanted a fresh perspective on how to lead leaders, so I approached my manager for guidance and suggestions. My manager ran the entire west coast and had extensive experience leading others. I told him about my first interaction and set up time to review what happened, provide my thoughts on how to fix the situation, and get his suggestions for improvement. (Note: You never want to bring up a problem without offering a recommended solution.)

My manager asked a lot of questions to gain an understanding of the situation. He said I needed to focus on the outcomes of the business and leave the details on how it comes together to the director. It was okay to offer coaching, but it needed to be focused on the director so they could, in turn, coach their own team. If I coached the team, then it took authority and responsibility away from the director, which would hinder the team's growth and development.

He said, "John, your job is to coach the coach, not the player. When things are not going according to plan, call a time out and have the team huddle to make sure they are all on the same page." I really appreciated that coaching and advice. I made a pivot at that point to do just that. It wasn't easy because that wasn't what I was used to doing, but over time it got easier and helped me tremendously in future roles.

In my next role, I was promoted to a senior vice-president position with a larger territory and more people. My previous manager was now my peer. Early on in this role, people took my suggestions or brainstorming as something I wanted them to implement. Sometimes this turned out well, but other times it wasted a lot of effort that wasn't beneficial to the person or the business. I had to be more careful about how I shared possibilities with people. But if I shared potential pitfalls or challenges about an idea, it could block pathways for new, innovative approaches.

During a leadership training class, I found a technique to encourage new thinking but also ask the person to do some additional reflection on how to navigate opportunities or challenges. It's a technique called, "I like, I like, but…"

When someone shares an idea, focus on the things you like best about it first and then point out something for them to consider. The beauty of this approach is that it keeps the idea alive without shutting it down. The person walks away with positive things to build on but a realistic view of what still needs to be solved. The person with the idea is still in charge and moving forward. Nothing is ever perfect, but if an idea is shut down, it never has the chance to morph into something new and improved.

I've learned that a core idea can be good, but sometimes, it might need further refinement on the details. You want people to keep working on an idea, to stay open, and use creative thinking. This technique required me to listen to ideas with a focus on what was positive or intriguing. I had to listen to what was good in the idea. It didn't mean I had to ignore the parts I didn't align with, but it did improve the tone of the conversation and how it ended.

Simply follow this formula: "I like this about your idea. I also like this other element. Can you tell me more about this?" The "tell me more" allows you to voice your concerns. For example, someone might want to improve your employee recognition program. Their idea is to give out gift cards for doing a good job. Your response might be, "I really like the idea of improving the employee recognition program. We need that right now, especially given the change and pace of the business. I like giving people something for doing a good job. Tell me more about how this would fit into our existing recognition program."

The person would need to further consider their idea. Maybe there are budget issues or other programs that should be replaced. Whatever the issues are, this approach allows the conversation to continue. You could ask them to give this additional consideration for the next discussion.

This approach is much better than, "We can't add a new element to our existing program right now." It keeps ideas open, doesn't shut down creativity, and allows people to solve the actual barriers to improvement. Having them continue to own and work the idea also presents an opportunity for growth for them instead of you just handling it. Shining a LIGHT on the concern still allows the person to take their shot to make it better.

Summary

It's important to have relationships with coaches who believe in you and encourage you to keep taking shots. You miss 100% of the shots you never take. When you lead people, it's critical to make the shift from focusing on yourself to focusing on others. You need to support and encourage others to keep taking their shot for everyone to be successful.

As a leader, you must set the vision and let others strive towards that vision. You get work done with and through others, not just yourself. There aren't enough hours in a day to do it all yourself. A strong leader focuses on outcomes and lets others determine how to get the work done.

Chapter Questions

1. How would you describe your current leadership style? What changes do you want to make? Does your team know you believe in them?
2. When you give constructive feedback, do you remember to deliver it with a positive comment, then constructive change, and finish with positive feedback so that the feedback can best be received?
3. Are you reaching out to your coaching network for advice or tips for your personal or business life? Who else could you connect with to learn more about how they tackle the challenges you are working on? Are you building your network outside of your own division or company to learn new approaches?

Chapter 13: Interviewing

Interviewing is one of the most important business skills to master. Having a good interview coach can mean the difference between landing a job or not. I've had a lot of experience interviewing on both sides of the table and learned some valuable lessons.

Preparation Meets Opportunity

One of the key elements to capturing an opportunity is making sure you have a strategy and are always prepared. In the spring of my senior year of college, I was planning to graduate and start my career in corporate America. Fortune 500 companies visited campus to recruit graduating seniors.

At my university, we had a bidding system to get the interviews. Each week we were given 1,000 points to bid on interviews. We could divide the points into allocations of 100. My strategy was to bid all 1,000 points on one interview per week so I could not be out-bid. I could tie someone with the same strategy but never be out-bid.

That spring, I interviewed with several consumer goods companies with mutual interest on both sides. I had an initial interview in which one company held a question-and-answer session in the late afternoon before the actual interviews the next morning. I didn't know if I was going to attend this informational session because I was playing pool with my friend Ricky at a local billiard hall. At the last minute, I cut my game short and attended. It may have been one of the best decisions of my life.

When I got to the lobby of the small room, I saw a young, professional man in a suit and tie. I introduced myself to the representative and made pleasant small talk, something that came naturally from my days as rush chairman at my fraternity. As the program began, the representative talked about the company, the job they were hiring for, and how the process was going to work. If we made it past this round, we would be flown to Chicago for a final round of interviews with candidates from other Midwest colleges. Right then, my goal was to make it to Chicago.

After the program was over, I shook hands with the representative and let him know I was looking forward to tomorrow and learning more about him and his company.

I got up the next morning and put on my standard interview attire: a charcoal grey suit, white pressed shirt, burgundy tie, and freshly polished black wingtip shoes. I grabbed my portfolio and pen and headed over to the student union where the interviews took place.

I waited in the reception area for my turn. When my name was called, I shook hands with the same representative who conducted the question-and-answer session the afternoon before. We already had a good connection from the day before. I was comfortable and at ease. The conversation just flowed.

The last part of the interview was a simulated selling situation. I was given a two-page handout, instructed to read it for five minutes, and then told to sell the interviewer based on the handout. The fictional company was "Sparkle Soda," and we had to pitch the idea of selling more of this product.

I read through the information in the document. I knew from some of my communication classes I had to core it down to 3 to 4 key ideas to stay on track. I wanted to gather more information, so I made sure I had prepared one or two questions to ask to gain more insight. I also said to myself, "Just be yourself and have fun with it." I relaxed and smiled.

I worked at being thoughtful, had a plan for the points I wanted to cover, and in the end, asked for the sale. Some of these things were concepts I learned in school, and others were shaped by my early jobs. Every experience we have shapes our lives based on where we are at that point in time.

As I concluded the mock sales pitch, the interviewer said I did well, and I should expect to receive a call and information about going to the final round in Chicago. He then gave me some insights on what to expect and how that process would play out. I was ecstatic! Now that I had advanced, it was important to learn more about this company and opportunity.

I received the call confirming I was advancing to the final round in Chicago. I was so excited that they were going to pay to fly me there and stay in a fancy hotel overnight. I read through the agenda for the interview day and noticed it included a math test based on the industry. Given my disdain for math, I was concerned. I needed to study and be ready.

I asked friends who I knew were good in math and analytics to help me think about certain questions and how to look for key words in a business case to focus on the most important elements. I also knew a cute girl who was very good at math, who later became my wife. She and I sat at the airport in Lincoln,

Nebraska, studying together while waiting for my flight. They announced it was time to board, and I gave her a kiss and a hug. When I reached Chicago, I made it to my hotel and went to bed early to ensure I was rested and ready for the interview of my life.

The next morning, I arrived at the office building to find several other college seniors waiting. When they shared the names of the prestigious schools and business programs they attended, it put me back on my heels. I wasn't even a business major. I was a speech communication major.

I questioned if I was in over my head or even able to compete. But I thought back to my high school basketball coach who told me to keep taking my shot, and that put me in a positive mindset that I could compete and win the day. Funny how those moments stick with you for a lifetime.

I took the industry-related math test first. It wasn't easy, but the coaching and advice I had received helped with questions about equipment requirements, finished ounces in product formulations, financial analysis, market research, and other topics. I thought I did well but knew it would be the area with my lowest score.

Next were several interviews, including a mock interview to sell a shoe to an executive with the company. I took a similar approach as I did with the Sparkle Soda mock sales pitch. I asked questions and made my case based on what I knew. At the end, I asked for the sale. Asking for the sale was a concept I knew from my days running my own painting business.

At the end of the day, the company said they would contact us in the next several weeks to let us know if we'd receive an offer. I flew back to Lincoln, Nebraska that night, and my girlfriend picked me up at the airport. It was a relief to be finished and wait to see where life would take me.

A couple of weeks later, I was sitting in the TV room of my fraternity house when a younger member said I had a telephone call. This was back in the day when we had one phone for over 70 guys in the fraternity house. I picked up the phone in the small phone room, and a woman with a southern accent was on the other line. She said, "John, we are very pleased to offer you a job as a Territory Sales Manager."

I was thrilled! She gave me the details of the offer: starting salary in the low 20s, company vehicle, and vacation that started the following year. The one caveat was they couldn't tell me the city I would start in because they didn't know which territories would be open when I started. It could be anywhere in the country.

I wrote down the details and asked when I needed to let them know because I had other offers I was considering. She said they needed to know within two weeks.

I thanked her, stepped out of the phone room, and screamed for joy! From bidding my 1,000 points per week to multiple offers in about ten weeks felt great. Now it was just about which offer to accept.

I narrowed my best offers down to two companies. Both were globally recognized in the consumer goods space. One would place me in Cincinnati, and the other city was unknown. Both had competitive salaries and benefit plans. I felt comfortable with each hiring manager. I debated both offers. I discussed the pros and cons with mentors.

In the end, I went with the offer from the company that paid the most. It was only $1,000 more than the other offer. Even though it probably wasn't the best way to decide, it worked out well as I spent over 32 years with that company. But it never would have happened if I hadn't seized the opportunity and made sure I was prepared for each of those interviews.

Tough Love

Sometimes you need someone to give feedback in the form of tough love. If you internalize it and make meaningful changes, it can benefit you more than when someone simply says you were really good. It's important to ask for feedback and determine what, if anything, you want to do with it. This is especially important when it comes to interviewing.

Five years into my first leadership role, I hit a point where I kept interviewing for vice president of sales positions but was never selected. I panicked over being stuck in a role and not achieving my long-term career goals. Out of desperation, I applied for positions that weren't a fit. I knew it wasn't the right approach, but I needed some advice on how to re-think my next career step.

I interviewed for a vice president of sales role out East. I felt good going into the interview. I knew the hiring manager, and I had examples with strong results from my current role. On the day of the interview, I went into the office with my best suit, tie, and polished shoes. I felt confident and ready.

During the interview, the hiring manager probed into my examples to determine the impact I had in my previous roles. He asked how far into the organization had my initiatives been implemented beyond my direct team. Had others adopted my idea in other parts of the country?

I had not done those things, but I knew I was doing a good job in my role and those would come later if given the opportunity to showcase them. Unfortunately, that thinking limited my growth and was not what the hiring manager or the panel was looking for in a leader of leaders.

About two weeks after the interview, the hiring manager called me. He said, "John, do you want to advance in the company?"

I said, "Of course I do. Otherwise, I wouldn't be posting for these roles."

He then instructed me to take out a sheet of paper, write down his feedback, and refer to it after the conversation. He explained that I did a good job, but with my current examples and experiences, I wasn't going to advance. He said my examples lacked impact to the broader organization. The people who were advancing had these types of experiences, whereas I did not. My current experiences weren't going to get me out of Triple A and into the Majors. As a sports fan, I related to his analogy.

I asked for his advice on how to advance. He said I needed to take on developmental projects or assignments that would show I could lead a larger group with strong, tangible results that impacted the business beyond my direct team.

I asked how I could do that while working in a smaller, remote market. He said that wasn't his problem and was up to me to figure out if I really wanted to advance.

I hung up the phone and felt conflicted. On one hand, I really appreciated the honest and actionable feedback. On the other hand, I didn't see a clear path to how I was going to accomplish what I needed to work on to grow and to achieve my career aspirations.

I sat on this feedback for a couple of weeks, unsure what to do with it. The time gave me a chance to reflect and think about several options where I could take on more responsibility in my current role. I was at a stage in my current position where I knew how to do the job and had some additional capacity.

I also shared the feedback with my manager, and he was very supportive of helping me. He said he'd keep an eye out for assignments that would help fill some of my current gaps versus my career goals.

A few months later, a development opportunity arose. The NCAA Final Four basketball tournament was coming to St. Louis, my home market, and they needed a leader to run the local activation for the system. They asked if I was interested in the opportunity. I couldn't believe how much it aligned with my passion for basketball and my desire to lead a broad and diverse group in the business. It also connected me to other people at our global headquarters. This was my shot!

The assignment was challenging. I studied what the local committee did the previous year in San Antonio. I built a cross-functional group of people that represented the various segments of our business. I built a budget with targets for consumer touchpoints, customer interaction, and community give-back opportunities.

One of our first reviews of the plan did not go well. I received some tough feedback from the Senior Vice President in charge of the program. Instead of taking it personally, I leaned in to learn more about his perspective and expectations. I set up regular check-ins with senior leaders to stay on track and meet our milestone objectives. This alignment allowed everyone to be on the same page before the tournament even started.

The tournament weekend was action-packed. Each 15-minute block was planned, and we had multiple meetings, market tours, and customer interactions. I barely had time to watch or even enjoy the games.

When the buzzer for the championship game sounded, I was relieved and exhausted, but I knew it had all gone well. I had made a difference and learned so much during this nine-month process. I received some very good feedback and got to interact with people I never would have met unless I raised my hand for this new opportunity. This taught me a valuable lesson about being open to tough feedback and saying yes to new opportunities and activities.

Four months after the Final Four, I saw a job posting on the company's internal site for a vice president of sales position on the West Coast. I talked to my wife about the opportunity. We weighed the pros and cons. We had young kids who were very established in their schools and our local community. We made the decision together to put my name in the hat and see if I would be selected for a face-to-face interview.

As the weeks progressed, I heard from many internal colleagues that this was going to be a very competitive pool. More than 40 internal candidates applied for the position, including many existing vice presidents, and my former manager was in the pool. It was going to take the interview of my life to win the day.

It was exciting to receive a call from human resources that I had made it to the face-to-face interview round in California.

Create Confidence

This interview felt different. I was calm and confident. I knew in my head and heart that I could perform well in this new role, and I could deliver exceptional results. The work on my development plan and efforts to take on outside activities gave me the experience I lacked in my previous interviews. I had taken the advice to heart and worked for over a year on building my skills.

I also set in motion an influencing strategy of people in my network to make calls or send notes to the hiring manager regarding my ability to perform this role at a high level. I reached out to people who would be my peers to introduce myself and let them know I had applied for the job and hoped we would have the opportunity to work with them in the future.

The interviews included a panel of two or three people that supported the hiring manager. The panel asked a series of questions based on skills for the role using a STAR format: Situation, Task, Action, and Results. Candidates were required to demonstrate the depth and breadth of current work and beyond, indicating the potential for additional responsibility and growth.

A few days before the interview, I received the logistical information, which included the usual details including the date, time, and location.

What caught my attention immediately was who was going to be on the panel besides the hiring manager. It was the senior leader who ran the Final Four event in St. Louis that I had reported to during my time leading that event. I knew him, he knew my work, and we had an instant connection when I walked into the interview room.

Taking on stretch assignments and putting myself out there never paid off more than in this situation. It wasn't going to get me the job. I still had to win the day against smart and talented people. But it was a big help for me and my confidence.

Belief in yourself and confidence are critical aspects for you when you are looking at doing something new and different. You don't have to know the path, but you need to know you can navigate the path with LIGHT shining and helping you succeed.

The day of the interview started like so many of my other interviews. I thought about my first interview back in Chicago and how far I had come. So many things had changed in my life, yet I put on my best suit, ironed my interview shirt, tied my red power tie, and shined my shoes.

As I made my way up the elevator in the Irvine office, I felt a sense of calm that I hadn't in my previous vice-president interviews. I was ready and had done the work to compete, but more importantly, to win the day.

The interviews went well. Much like the interviews over a year ago, a lot of the follow-up questions surrounded the impact I had beyond the examples given. This time I had specific, measurable answers and examples. I painted a picture of how I could make an immediate impact on the people and business in this expanded role. The conversation was easy, and it flowed. I was relaxed but confident.

When I had my second interview with the person I worked under for the Final Four event, it was again like when we were working together. I knew him. I knew his style. When I talked about the impact I had on the March Madness event, he already knew about it in detail. I also talked about how I hadn't won past positions for which I'd interviewed, but that I took the feedback to heart and implemented it to improve. It showed I was coachable and willing to do the work to advance.

After the interview, I received a call from the hiring manager. I held my breath as he said, "John, I would like to offer you the job of Vice President of Sales in the West." I was elated. I was barely able to say, "I accept." I took down the notes of the offer, start date, and other details. I ended the call and went to tell my wife we were headed west. When I told her, she cried. She cried happy tears for us but also sad tears for leaving friends and a community that we built over time. These decisions and moves impact your family and others around you in profound ways.

Summary

Interviewing requires many strategies and skills. You need to understand the role and reasons why you are interested in the position. How do the job requirements match up to your current skills? What are your gaps, and how do you overcome them with the hiring manager or interview panel? Are you working to expand your relationships and knowledge through new experiences that will benefit you in the future?

You need to understand the process and flow of the interview and how to put yourself in the best position to not only answer the question but to win the job. Can the hiring manager see you in this role or opportunity? How are you using your network to let others know and assess your readiness to take on this new role? It is important to put in the work and time to assess these areas before you post for a job. Take your time to look at this role and see if it really makes sense for you. If it does, take your shot.

Chapter Questions
1. How does a new role play into your career journey? Do you have a career journey? If not, plan out the next five, ten, or even twenty years of your working career to see where you want to go.
2. What are you working to build your skills and experiences? If the answer is nothing, then create some time and capacity for new skills. Developing new skills prevents you from becoming stuck in your current state.
3. Do you have a network of people that you can seek out for career advice? Make a list of those relationships and let them know you want to connect and share your current thinking on your career and see what advice they may have for you.
4. Are you volunteering or giving back to others? This is a great way to meet new people, build new skills, and give back to your community. Don't wait for the perfect opportunity. Just start and see where it may take you.

Chapter 14: The Girl in High School

I remember passing Alisa Marie Wade in the hallway at Westside High School in Omaha, Nebraska, in the fall of 1981. She was wearing a cheerleading uniform as she cheered for the varsity sports teams. At the time, our first year of attending high school was our sophomore year. Middle school included grades seven through nine. Only four sophomore girls made the varsity cheerleading squad, so as a teenage boy in high school, you knew who they were.

Alisa and I didn't hang out in the same circle of friends or have any classes together during our first two years at Westside. I played basketball, so I would see her on the sidelines cheering, but we kept to our separate orbits of life. That all changed the summer before our senior year of high school.

I was attending a basketball camp at the University of Nebraska in Lincoln, and Alisa was attending a camp for academics on campus at the same time. I remember running into her as we were headed to the campus cafeteria. She was on break from her camp, and the basketball campers were headed to lunch. It was a hot and humid summer day in the Midwest, and I was drenched in sweat from the morning session of basketball camp.

When I saw her, I smiled and said hi. She smiled back and asked how my summer was going. This was my shot to talk to her.

I asked if she wanted to join me for lunch with my camp roommate, Gus. She accepted, and we sat down for lunch. It was the first time we had an extended conversation, and I thought she was cute, smart, and funny. I was really smitten with her and asked if I could call her when we got back home to Omaha. She said yes, and I followed up on it after we got back.

The Simple Things in Life

Alisa and I have been together since 1983, and we have been married since 1991. I have been with her for almost 70% of my life.

We have two adult children, Steven and Emily. One of the things younger couples ask us is how we have stayed together and have been married for 30 years. We both laugh and smile, but we know the cliché answer: we are best friends.

We love doing everyday things together. I am not here to say that marriage doesn't take a lot of work and commitment, but you need to be able to enjoy each day with your spouse or partner. You need to find joy and happiness in the day. That will change with careers, kids, activities, and life in general, but you must work, communicate, and find things you each enjoy doing with the other person. I am not talking about big expensive things; I am talking about the small, simple things.

For example, one of our mutual passions is cooking. We love to plan, prepare, cook, and enjoy a meal together. One of our favorite things is to cook on Saturday night together. This mutual activity starts much earlier in the week than Saturday. We sit down and talk about what we want to make later in the week.

I love to grill, and many times, it will be some sort of steak. We love going to an open farmer's market in the summer and talking to the various vendors about what's fresh or in season. We plan our side dishes based on their recommendations. We love to hear about their businesses, farms, and what inspires them to set up a tent in the middle of summer in Texas.

We then go to a local butcher and see what they have in the case and talk about the cut and grade of meat available that day. We might end the day at a local wine shop and ask for recommendations based on what we purchased and what can pair well with the food we'll be cooking.

We love to go home and put on some music as we prepare the meal. We might listen to music from our roots in the 80s or some jazz. We go out to the grill and share some wine and talk about our day or what is going on in our lives.

It's a time when things slow down that we connect, listen, and catch up with each other. We then sit down and enjoy our meal together. (Hey guys, one more coaching tip is you should take care of the dishes!) I still love connecting with Alisa just like we did the first time we talked in the college cafeteria that summer in '83.

I asked Alisa to give her take on how we first met so you can hear from both of us.

Alisa: John's rendition of us meeting in high school is slightly off. He gives a perception that I didn't TOTALLY know who he was from our sophomore year. I knew he was the only one in our grade who made the varsity basketball team that year. He was so cute and tall!

John was very good friends with a mutual friend, Chris, who I worked with in journalism, and I would see them in the halls. We even had a class together our junior year.

Our high school prepared us for college with large group lecture halls for classes with science labs. All students taking the class that semester would have one period of lecture together. For physics that spring, I made it to my assigned seat in the large theater early just so I could see John and his friends come in laughing a few minutes later. Anyone who has heard John, or for that matter his brother, Brian, laugh knows that laugh alone will make you smile.

That scorching Nebraska summer afternoon at camp ahead of our senior year is still so vivid in my mind even 38 years later. John was dripping in sweat coming out of basketball practice. What he doesn't realize is how HOT I thought it made HIM look!

As we approached the door of the dorm cafeteria, I can still hear myself thinking, "OMG, that is JOHN SATTEM!" I had never been bold enough to even talk to him before. And then he looked at me with those great eyes, smiled in a way that melted my 16-year-old girl's heart, and said, "Hi."

I couldn't believe it when he asked me to join him for lunch! Still, to this day, I am grateful that I said yes. Laughing with Gus and John at lunch started a ton of fun times, and a great, deep friendship between John and I was born.

Communication and friendship have always been the pillar of our relationship. We could talk and talk. So much so that our first year of college away from each other, we had HUGE long-distance phone bills as John and I spent hours together on the phone each week.

Those talks led to a deeper understanding with a lot of laughter sprinkled in. So, pay attention if there is someone who you love talking to for hours.

And John is right; we are each other's best friend. No one knows each other better. And yes, it hasn't always been easy. But going back to what bonds your friendship and what you enjoy doing together helps you appreciate everyday life more. So, if you are ever feeling off with someone who is important to you, ask yourselves what you did when you were having fun. We do love cooking together and listening to music. We love it when a great song comes on while we are prepping dinner, and we might even dance in our kitchen together, which can be pretty funny. But smiling together, talking, and just connecting in our home is a great night.

Couple Time

This is for all the moms and dads who are in the crazy-busy years of your kids' activities. For Alisa and me, this was most of our late 30s and all of our 40s.

We have two great kids, and we wanted to make sure we supported them in school, sports, and outside activities. The kids were involved in swimming, football, soccer, basketball, and scouting. Both of them were excellent students in a highly competitive public school system in Colorado.

Alisa and I were involved in some form or fashion in many of these activities. I coached basketball and football. Alisa was the team manager for the neighborhood swim team. She was also a cub scout leader and a manager for our daughter's travel-soccer team.

We divided and conquered between school and getting the kids to their practices and games. We met amazing people through these experiences and rode the waves up and down on wins, losses, and tryouts each year. Lifelong friendships were born from these relationships for all four of us.

We really enjoyed watching our kids compete, build new skills, learn life lessons, and make great friends. However, if there is one piece of advice that we could share with anyone during this stage in life, it is to not lose sight of how important being a married couple is during this time.

Looking back, we didn't make the time for just the two of us to get away for a long weekend. You don't even need to leave your city to make this happen. For many years, we didn't have any immediate family living in the same city, but we always had a great network of friends who were willing to help. We just didn't make it a priority. We went from our 20th wedding anniversary to our 25th without a dedicated trip for just the two of us. We could chalk it up to being busy with work, life, and other commitments, but those are just excuses. All of this changed when I moved to Dallas for my last role.

Alisa and I made the decision to commute for a year between Dallas and Denver while our daughter finished her senior year in high school. That time away from each other taught us a lot about our relationship. It taught me to appreciate all the things that Alisa did for our family and for me, including the amount of time and work that went into running our home and taking care of all the things around the house.

I did these things on my own while living in Dallas, and it took a lot of time and effort to accomplish even little tasks. I planned my work and free time around getting all this stuff done. It really taught me to appreciate her and our marriage more than ever.

Being apart for a year is difficult on a marriage or any other committed relationship. But it was also fun when Alisa came to Dallas for a weekend. It was like dating my wife all over again. We went out for dinners, saw concerts, explored cool places for Sunday brunch, and enjoyed fall football games.

One beautiful, sunny, crisp fall Sunday afternoon, we asked ourselves, "Why were we not doing this more before now?" We didn't have a good answer. We couldn't go back and change our past, but we knew we could change our future.

We made a commitment to take a couple's trip once per year and have a date night at least twice per month. It was easier because both kids were out of the house and in college or starting their careers, but it still took time and commitment.

If you are in a similar place as we were in our 40s, our best advice is to slow down and find a way to make your marriage the center of your family. If the marriage isn't strong, the rest of the family can't be as strong as possible. I am grateful we were able to LIGHT up our path forward.

Alisa: John is so right about this. It was great supporting the kids, and we both gained so much enjoyment from our involvement with their activities. Although, truth be told, being a cub master and giving a group of 7-year-old scouts knives to earn their merit badge was also a bit stressful.

In the midst of all these great activities, we still should have made spending quality time with just the two of us and our marriage more of a priority. It would have made life that much more fun. It is helpful to carve out time for each other when you aren't so tired or at the end of the day. And sometimes, during that busy phase of life with career demands and kids, it's hard to find that time or energy. But be creative.

Toward the end of our time in Colorado, we started going for a drive in the beautiful countryside and finding cute places to grab lunch or pull up a barstool and have a beer. Again, it gave us uninterrupted time to just talk and connect.

I would also take this concept one step further and say don't lose the connection with yourself. Take care of yourself.

As a stay-at-home mom, I battled that challenge. Sometimes I struggled to answer what it was I loved to do and what made me healthy physically, mentally, and spiritually.

It's important for your own happiness and joy in life. Make YOU a priority, which can be challenging with so many demands on your time. When you find joy in those demands, whether it is work or your kids, it can be easy to miss that you are not always taking care of yourself or the toll those roles take on you too. You need to be a priority so you can be better, period. But it will also make you a better partner and parent. As the saying goes, put your own oxygen mask on first.

It's great when your partner helps you do that too. Even if the driver always needs to be me in my own wellbeing, John's support on my path has been very impactful. Working out together and walking can be an excellent way to connect. It also has been great to be whisked away by my boyfriend/husband again. You really should not lose that role of boyfriend and girlfriend to each other. It brings joy and keeps the spark alive.

Make the effort. It will pay off! It also sets a good example for your children. I remember flying out to visit John in Dallas with our daughter, Emily, before we moved and joined him there. Denver International Airport requires a lot of walking, and I had worn flats. When the captain of our flight announced we were beginning our descent into Dallas, I grabbed my carry-on bag. While I whipped out heels, a brush, and lip gloss, Emily asked what I was doing.

I replied, "I don't get to see your dad that often right now. I want to look nice." And while being comfortable with each other in sweats and no make-up is great, there's a lot to be said for making a little effort sometimes too.

Ask for Help

One of the themes of this book is that "asking for help is a sign of strength, not a weakness." As we all know, 2020 was a hard year for many people. No one could have predicted the impact the pandemic would have on the entire world.

I was at a business conference in early March of 2020 and talked to an economist about the potential impact on the business I was leading. He said, "John, are you prepared to lose 20 to 30 percent, or even more of your business?" I stared at him in total disbelief. He said some models suggested this may happen. That was one of the first times I really contemplated what impact the virus could have on our lives.

I went to a business meeting in Dallas on March 18, 2020. The meeting felt strange. We used hand sanitizer as we entered the lobby of the building. We didn't shake hands. We gave some awkward hand gestures to start the meeting. We sat in a small huddle room to conduct the meeting. It was obvious everything was a little "off." People tried, but everyone's mind wandered to where things were going with the virus.

We walked out of the building, and I headed back to my office to get a few things because I was going to work from home the next day. I picked up a few items and stuffed them into my business bag. I turned off my office light. That was the last time I was in my office until I cleaned it out six months later when I decided to accept a voluntary severance package after 32 years and officially retire on November 15, 2020.

That year was also difficult for Alisa and me. I retired and had to chart what was going to be next for my professional career. Alisa had to deal with her dad battling cancer for the third time. Our kids moved back home for different periods of time. We missed special family celebrations and holidays. Alisa and I were forced to stop doing many of the things we loved doing together, such as going to church and out to brunch afterward.

We missed traveling and seeing other parts of the world. We missed live music and concerts. We missed spending time with family and friends.

But we also had some good things happen. We got to spend time and connect over family dinners. We spent more time taking walks and relishing a slower pace. I wasn't on a plane every week and could get into a new routine at home.

However, as the year went on, the uncertainty of life took a toll. Alisa's dad, Paul Wade, passed away on January 9, 2021. I started a new business and writing this book while adjusting to a new work-life schedule. Alisa and I both struggled with these things coming at us, and we knew things were "off" for us both individually and as a couple.

In the past, we would have put these challenges aside and mushed forward. As a family, we made our way to Omaha to bury Alisa's dad. It was very emotional. There were moments of sadness and tears, as well as moments of great memories and laughter.

I really admired how Alisa and her two brothers got through the week and then began the process of cleaning out and selling their family home of 52 years. Again, there were lots of tears but great memories as well.

When Alisa and I returned from the funeral, we sat down and shared how we were feeling about ourselves and our marriage. We made a commitment to seek professional help from a counselor. Alisa knew a person in Denver when we lived there who was available for virtual appointments. We scheduled individual sessions, shared what we wanted to work on and where we wanted to go.

It's important to be honest about what you are doing and what role you have when things aren't going as well as you would like. We met with the counselor on a regular basis, and it has helped us individually and as a couple. We share what we are working on and have incorporated some regular tools and techniques that are helping us navigate our way through this tough time.

I am not saying what we are doing will work for everyone, but it's important to slow down and reflect on what is getting in your way to see how someone can help you navigate through life. Everyone has challenges. Some are more out in the open and evident.

Here are five things that Alisa and I have found help us:

1. We pray every morning for help and guidance, as well as to show our gratitude to God.
2. I meditate each morning for ten minutes. This helps me slow down to start my day and gets me more grounded to take on what comes my way.
3. We get outside every day and pay more attention to the small things in our surroundings. We find beauty through God every day in places we never looked in the past.
4. We ask each other about our most important things in the day, and we support them to help make it happen. It's amazing what you can do when you actively listen and make your spouse's priority yours.
5. At the end of each week, we sit down without electronic devices and take turns sharing what was good in the week and what was challenging. We always end with gratitude. This has been a great way to connect, listen, appreciate,

and support each other. What you find is that a lot happens in only one week's time. Taking this time reminds you of the good in the week but also allows you to understand and address the challenges. Having uninterrupted time to just listen to each other has been powerful.

As I look back at this list, what has been helpful is having these tools and processes in place to help both of us navigate everyday life. Things will always come at us, but we are so much better prepared to handle them by focusing on those things together.

Alisa: I think almost everyone will look back at 2020 and 2021 as a difficult period of time with much loss and change. (Note: Our yellow lab, Aspen, would argue it's been great since she loves having everyone home so much. So, it may be perspective.) But life does throw waves at you. Sometimes you will not even see it coming, and it may knock you off your feet.

I think one takeaway John and I have from this last bit of time is when you hit a stretch with a lot of change or loss, pay attention. Don't try to just push through on your own. Sit with the pain and find a positive way to help process it. If you bury it, it doesn't really go away.

God has helped us. A counselor also helped us individually and as a couple. Family and friends have helped us. Just be real, embrace being vulnerable, and seek out support. Be there for each other and pay attention to yourself. Love wins!

Summary

If you find a best friend and you happen to fall in love with them, chances are you found the person for you. What I love about my marriage and relationship with Alisa is how much fun we have every day. Not every moment is fun, and everyone knows how hard some days can be, but I can't think of anyone else I would want to be on my life journey with other than Alisa. I am glad I took my shot and talked to her all those years ago.

Find joy in everyday things, and the big, exciting things will seem even better.

One piece of unsolicited advice I would give any young couple is to make your marriage the center point of your family. If it isn't strong, the rest will fray at the edges. You may or may not recognize it, but the frays will show themselves over time.

Last, getting help is important. You may have people helping you with so many aspects of your life including your physical, financial, and spiritual well-being. If you need help with your marriage, don't be afraid to seek it out. It can make a world of difference.

Chapter Questions
1. Does your spouse or significant other know what you love or admire about them? Ask, and if they don't know, tell them. Ask what they love or admire about you. It will be interesting to see where the conversation takes you.
2. What are you doing daily to make your marriage or relationship stronger? When was the last time you spent quality time together, just the two of you? What's getting in the way of that? How will you make it a priority? Shine a LIGHT on your challenges and take them head-on. It will give you strength and confidence to keep at in the future.
3. Are you in a rut with your spouse or partner? What is causing it? Are you taking care of your own health and wellness? Who can you seek out for guidance or help? Asking for help is a pathway to a potentially different outcome.

Closing Thoughts

Reflecting back, I see the importance of knowing when I needed help. Throughout my life, I changed my perspective and realized it was a sign of strength to ask for help. You don't need to go it alone. LIGHT your path using this simple framework:

Learn From Everyone

Invite Collaboration

Grow Your Knowledge and Skills

Healthy Relationships Matter

Take Your Shot

Don't let things get too far down the road or become overwhelming before you raise your hand for help. We all need it. Some of us are better at recognizing that earlier than others. Listen to yourself and know when it's time. It will bring you more happiness and fulfillment in life.

There are many paths in our lives: personal growth paths, career paths, relationship paths, health paths, and spiritual paths. Each path will need various levels of LIGHT to help guide you at different stages of your life. If you are seeking greater success at any stage, then pause, reflect and shine a LIGHT on your path. Be open, and you will see a new or better path to lead you to the success you want in your life.

Also realize the type of impact you have on others with your own coaching and leadership. In some cases, it may be small to help someone solve a problem. But every interaction has the possibility of having a beneficial impact on someone that changes their life in a profound way. Help LIGHT someone's path to success as others have done for you.

Shine LIGHT and strive for more happiness. That is true success. You need to believe in yourself and find others who believe in you when times are tough. You need people in your corner who see your potential but hold you accountable when you veer off or are not putting your best effort forward. Everyone grows best where it's LIGHT, so LIGHT your path to success. You can do this!

About the Author

During his 30+ year career in a Fortune 100 company, John Sattem rose from an entry-level sales position to the role of global Senior Vice President with over $1 Billion in annual sales. John gained a reputation as someone who consistently created a winning culture for his team members based upon empowerment and collaboration.

John and his wife, Alisa, live outside Dallas, Texas. Together, they have two children, Steven and Emily, as well as a yellow Labrador retriever, Aspen.

www.ingramcontent.com/pod-product-compliance
Lightning Source LLC
Chambersburg PA
CBHW031445040426
42444CB00007B/981